Praise for *Going On and On*

'A sharp slap to our complacency about the catastrophic damage we're wreaking on our planet, our economy, and the creative regeneration of our culture in refusing to accept that our lives must end. In *Going On and On*, the always brilliant Lucinda Holdforth presents a courageous, witty, compelling and often beautiful argument for my generation to hurry up and let go.

Her book has made me revise my own plans for growing old, showing me how to think clearly and compassionately about the gift we must give the future in supporting the young, stepping back and giving way.'

CHARLOTTE WOOD, Booker Prize-shortlisted author of *Stone Yard Devotional*

'Compelling, provocative and quite hilarious.'

JOE ASTON, bestselling author of *The Chairman's Lounge*

'A provocative and challenging contribution to the intergenerational debate.'

HUGH MACKAY, bestselling author of *The Way We Are*

GOING ON AND ON

Also by Lucinda Holdforth

True Pleasures: A memoir of women in Paris

Why Manners Matter: The case for civilised behaviour in a barbarous world

Leading Lines: How to make speeches that seize the moment, advance your cause and lead the way

21st-Century Virtues: How they are failing our democracy

GOING ON AND ON

WHY OUR LONGEVITY THREATENS THE FUTURE

Lucinda Holdforth

Summit Books Australia

GOING ON AND ON:
WHY OUR LONGEVITY THREATENS THE FUTURE

First published in Australia in 2026 by Summit Books Australia, an imprint of Simon & Schuster (Australia) Pty Limited
Level 4, 32 York Street, Sydney NSW 2000

Summit Books and colophon are trademarks of Simon & Schuster, LLC

10 9 8 7 6 5 4 3 2 1

Sydney/Melbourne New York Amsterdam/Antwerp London Toronto New Delhi
Visit our website at www.simonandschuster.com.au

A catalogue record for this book is available from the National Library of Australia

ISBN: 9781761821004

Cover design by Christabella Design/Christa Moffitt
Typeset by Midland Typesetters, Australia
Printed and bound in Australia by Griffin Press

The paper this book is printed on is certified against the Forest Stewardship Council® Standards. Griffin Press holds chain of custody certification SCS-COC-001185. FSC® promotes environmentally responsible, socially beneficial and economically viable management of the world's forests.

For Abigail and Rex and Laureleï and Lucian

It's fair to say that 80% of the world's problems involve old men hanging on, who are afraid of death and insignificance, and they won't let go.

Barack Obama
London, 25 September 2025

TABLE OF CONTENTS

INTRODUCTION: THE REVOLUTION IS HERE

Ours is the first cohort in history whose problem is not dying too young but living too long. For most of human history your average human being was dead before their 35th birthday. Yes, given high infant mortality rates, this was humanity's mortal paradigm for thousands of years. Even in the world's industrialising cities of 1870, the record shows that average life expectancy was a mere 30 years. From there, longevity began its steady ascent, but as recently as 1950 the average global life span was still only 46 years. Today that just gets you to your first midlife crisis. From 1950 on, with advances in infant and childhood health, peace and prosperity, improved diets, better sanitation and numerous medical breakthroughs, global life expectancy accelerated. It reached 73 years by 2019, a nine-year extension since 1990.

Australia is a starry performer in the global longevity firmament. In 1945, average Australian life expectancy at birth was 68 years; by 2019 it was 83. We are now firmly among the top ten most long-lived populations on the planet, sometimes ranked as high as third. Men aged 65 in 2023 can expect to live to 85 and women to 88. But that's just on average. We all know of people living longer. Sooner or later, dear reader, we *are* those people.

As a nation at the global forefront of this longevity revolution, we should be at the global forefront of thinking carefully and clearly about what longevity means and how we manage it. But no. Our politicians and policymakers freely admit that the longevity phenomenon is hugely significant for each of us as individuals and profound for our society. But so far, they have not faced up to the daunting challenge of presenting to us the full suite of implications and options that will help us manage this new world—including how we actively promote necessary generational change, where ageism may be justified and should be reinstated, and when and how we are allowed to die. Weighty reports are being written, but public commentary still swings dramatically between false cheer about the joys of 'positive ageing' and barely contained panic about how that promise can possibly be fulfilled without bankruptcy for us as individuals and a nation. This is no workable approach for the future.

If we want to be responsible citizens in this era of longevity, then developing a new, holistic and clarified way of thinking will be required. We won't be alone in tackling this challenge; many prosperous nations are affected by the same trend. But we should be prepared to take the lead on this because we *are* the lead.

In 2023 the Australian Government handed down the Intergenerational Report: Australia's future to 2063. This document describes the various issues bearing upon the Australian economy over the next 40 years and offers projections for the future. It lists population ageing first in its catalogue of the major issues we will face, ahead of climate change and the transformation to a net zero economy and looming geopolitical risks. It's that big.

What became clear to me on reading the report is that in any sphere requiring an economic solution over the next 40 years, longevity—our ageing population—will almost certainly be part of the problem. Often, it will be the whole problem. Nowhere, however, is this articulated out loud. A longer life is traditionally celebrated as a symbol of personal merit and societal achievement. Who wants to declare that living longer is a *problem* for our economy and for our society?

I'm putting up my hand.

And it's clearly there in the report, which acknowledges that a future with a smaller share of working-age Australians will result in lower revenues, even as 'expenditure on age-related government services, such as health and aged care, subsidised superannuation, the Age Pension, and end-of-life support is expected to increase'. It goes on, 'Around 40% of the projected increase in Australian Government expenditure from 2022–2023 to 2062–63 is due to demographic ageing.' *Forty per cent.* That's a confronting prediction, to say the least.

Greg Jericho and David Richardson of the Australia Institute noted that this future would require Australia to move from being a comparatively low-taxing nation to a far higher-taxing one if we were to support the aged care needs of the nation. They cautioned against undue alarm about this. Sweden, they pointed out, has close to the same old age-dependency ratio today as Australia is expected to have by 2063 and enjoys almost the same level of GDP per capita. The difference, however, is that the Swedish government raises around 43 per cent of GDP worth of revenue annually compared to the Australian government raising just 28 per cent.

So let us think of the future spending that, because of the demands of longevity, may *not* be targeted towards the needs of the future Australia. That means less money spent on major priorities such as child care and early education and paid parental leave that encourages women to have children. Or investments necessary to support education and higher education, science and innovation. The outlays required to shift us to a carbon net zero economy and deal with the extreme weather events that climate change is already causing. Better community health programs. National defence in a dangerous world. Measures to support Australia's cultural strength and social cohesion, including the arts and sport. Instead, all those taxpayer dollars will be spent keeping more and more old people going on. And on.

The current discourse around the ageing population seeks to normalise longevity. As if this is just another incremental change that Australian society will gradually adjust to, in the same way that earlier generations adjusted to the dangerous miracle of cars by building highways and making traffic rules. But this is not a matter of incremental change. It's a huge and transformational societal change that we haven't squarely faced, let alone internalised.

This essay is about longevity and its downsides, its many shades of blue. It's about the tough questions our new, unprecedented longevity asks us about life, about money, about illness and death, and intergenerational duty.

It's also about the positive guidance offered to us by history, should we choose to take note. Human progress in developed societies over hundreds of years has always relied on risk, daring and an appetite for change. And this, as I will not fail to remind you in the following pages, is overwhelmingly the province of the young. Whether you look at politics, science, technology or culture, the revolutionary jumps have been driven by the generational turnover of power, ideas and attitudes. It's the story of age yielding to youth, stasis giving way to movement, the past giving way to the future.

So what does it mean when our democratic society today is skewed by demographics, culture and law in favour of the interests of old people? And what will happen in this, our astonishing, unprecedented age of longevity, when the cohort of old people has never been bigger or more politically powerful, and when the passing of the generational baton is ever longer deferred?

Well, we can fairly assume that *less* happens. Less change, less movement, less action. The old will always be the population cohort whose interests lie in the near term not the long term; whose pride is invested not in what they might dare to achieve, but what they have already accomplished. As George Bernard Shaw put it in *Heartbreak House*, 'Old men are dangerous: it doesn't matter to them what is going to happen to the world'.

Change is never automatically a good thing, of course. But we can be fairly sure that any society ruled by its elders for a long period of time is as doomed to failure as the mad gerontocracy of the ancient Greek city-state of Sparta that once thrived but abruptly disappeared. We are now in a historical moment that requires concerted change. Hard policy decisions must be made in order to mitigate the future threats and present impacts of climate change; reorient our society away from the extreme inequality of the neoliberal economic model towards a more equitable and sustainable capitalism (that thereby sustains and strengthens democracy); and manage the overwhelming economic and social impact of longevity itself, including the burden it places on families and especially women. These are challenges requiring energetic commitment to the future, not incremental steps based on the past.

The issues are interrelated. Neoliberalism favours private enterprise. It has led to a big economic and societal shift, with the ownership and provision of many public services transferred from the government to the private sector. With an accompanying bias towards lower corporate taxes and less tax on wealth, this leaves less money for social good. The rich are therefore much richer, and have more power and influence across more spheres of our society. But for the many, permanent jobs have been converted to uncertain gigs, tertiary education is a luxury, and secure affordable housing is hard to come by. This has made us into a far more divided society, one that is now structured to make most of us feel more like anxious subjects than confident citizens. For many, an elongated old age in a society with a declining social support system will feel more like something to fear than celebrate. For the young, the future looks less like a wide horizon of opportunity than an obstacle course blocking the way to a good job, secure housing, opportunity or advancement. Meanwhile, they will inherit an Australia subject to the shocks and costs of climate change and its mitigation, a crisis that their parents have failed to address. Ken Henry, a former Treasury secretary and chair of the Australian Climate and Biodiversity Foundation, has openly described the failure to improve our nation's environmental management as 'a wilful act of intergenerational bastardry'.

We have an opportunity to manage Australian longevity better than this. To do so, we need to ensure that our health system is reoriented away from preserving life at any price to an updated model of helping people live well and die well too. Our 'anti-ageism' policies appear benevolent, but there are valid arguments on safety grounds as well as broader social benefit for reinstating qualified ageism in some arenas. We must at all costs strive to give younger Australians their shot at shaping the future to achieve progress. Equally, in this country that prides itself on fairness, we must ensure that ageing Australians are sufficiently supported, both economically and socially, to endorse that necessary transfer of power.

INTRODUCTION: THE REVOLUTION IS HERE

We are the first cohort in human history that is called upon to think consciously and act deliberately to promote timely generational change. It is a great human task.

LIFE AS MARATHON

Let's start with what it means to live an Australian life today. It's not what it used to be. Life used to be a sprint; now it's more like a marathon. This represents a fundamental challenge to the way we are each obliged to plan, sequence and finance our individual lives. It's a gigantic psychological and emotional job as much as a financial and practical one. For those of us of a certain age today, it requires changing gears mid-race, rewriting our life plans to last the long, long haul to the ever-receding finish line.

Personally, I fear and deplore the prospect of an incapacitated and, based on the statistics, possibly demented old age. More than this, at age 63, I doubt I can afford to live for another 30 or, God forbid, 40 years, even in the relatively modest manner to which I have never become accustomed, and especially with the very rational expectation of a long, debilitated tail end of life, with its varying degrees of medical and aged care expenses. When I look at my preferred social barometer of modern anxiety, LinkedIn, I see today the false bravado of so many 60- and 50-somethings who have either lost their job and can't find another (blaming it, rightly or wrongly, on 'ageism'), or choose not to step back, despite growing stale over many years in their senior role. All are afraid of loss of income, security or status.

But even if I could afford a super-elongated life span, and even if I wasn't demented, I'm not sure I would want it. I am surely not alone. Many Australians today will have their own reservations about the prospect of limitless-seeming longevity.

Meanwhile, younger people—by younger I mean those in their twenties and thirties, (or even forties and fifties and isn't that a sign of the times)—will be more preoccupied by the longevity of their parents. Like the indebted children desperately awaiting an inheritance to pay the mortgage or get one in the first place. Or the army of stressed and weary daughters, in a state of constant readiness for the next crisis to befall one or more of their 80- or 90-something parents, while managing their own health issues, raising or supporting their own children, and sometimes helping to raise their grandchildren too: the so-called sandwich generation.

The biggest victims of modern longevity, of course, are the expanding, often lonely and sad cohort of the old aged themselves. They may be struggling along timidly or bravely in their homes for as long as they can, supported by visits from harried family members or intermittent community carers, only to find their survival rewarded with the humiliations of prolonged old age, drifting in and out of memory and boredom in pastel chairs in the old people's homes, eating tasteless mush, sleeping on meagre narrow beds. For many in these circumstances, longevity is not what they crave; they've had more than enough of it. Their friends have died, their children need to live their own lives, they feel in their brittle bones that their time has passed. But they are being kept alive by a medical system that is brilliant at setting people up to lead a low quality of life for a very long time, waiting with dismal resignation for it all to end. For many it feels less like extended living than a cruel prolongation of the process of death. Which, in fact, it is.

As I write this, armadas of clever people are making it all but inevitable that we Australians will see our lives extended still further. Scientists around the world, including leading researchers here, are hunting down the secrets of extreme longevity, if not eternal youth. Advances in medical science, plus our own well-informed behavioural changes, will ensure this comes to pass. In the absence of smoking and drug or alcohol abuse, with the right diet, exercise programs, and attention to mental health and mental acuity, many people are now living well into their nineties.

What's more, if you aren't exercising hard and eating sparsely and taking your supplements, if you aren't testing and measuring and monitoring yourself with obsessive self-fascination, and buying all the latest longevity products and services, if you don't aim to cross a vigorous 100-year finish line, you are increasingly seen as lacking some core human quality. Ambition, perhaps. Self-discipline. It seems to me that consumerism has lined up with modern narcissism and its shadow side, social anxiety, to push the notion that outliving all your peers will somehow prove you are a better, more worthy, class of human. I have no idea why.

And the irony is that even as you make the effort to combat the physical and mental effects of ageing through dietary changes and exercise and fresh air and social connections, that probably won't be enough to satisfy the culture of the modern job market, where it's frowned upon to look or dress your age, unless that age is permanently, say, 35 or 40. Think of all the money and time and effort and personal angst we are expending on that.

The French philosopher Simone de Beauvoir once wrote a long treatise on the agony of old age. She was a self-aware French woman who was unafraid to say she hated ageing because of what it was doing to her appearance. For de Beauvoir, growing old wasn't natural and right; it was something horrible that happened to you without your consent. In *The Coming of Age*, published in 1970 when she was 62, she described her feeling of alienation as she looked at that unrecognisable old woman in the mirror. Her discomfort was magnified when she observed other people looking at this sadly altered Simone—scrutinising and, no doubt, judging her ageing face. It was a double alienation. For de Beauvoir, sustaining her self-image, her 'authentic subjectivity', as she grew older was simply 'unrealisable'.

As I was reading de Beauvoir's words, I was suddenly reminded of my nanna who, in the 1970s, represented a very different kind of ageing woman. After our family's eight-hour drive she would greet us at her farm gate for the annual Christmas visit with wide open arms and a deep enveloping hug. She would have been filling the pantry, stocking up the whisky, laying fresh sheets on beds and designating which of her calves and kittens and pups were most worthy of her grandchildren's admiration. She smoked and drank and played the piano; rode horses in her youth and drove a rattling Holden station wagon in her old age. To us her wrinkles were irrelevant, her soft upper arms and powdery old-lady smell meant comfort, and that dashing swipe of bright pink lipstick told of her joy in our arrival. Nanna represented continuity, constancy and a deep radical acceptance of herself and others. To all her grandkids she was model of wholeness, the very antithesis of alienation.

Today, of course, depending on how you look at it, a modern de Beauvoir is either set free, or forced by society, to envisage a very different kind of longevity. Because now you *can* eradicate all those signs of ageing—or defer them indefinitely, at least. Old age in its traditional guise doesn't even have to happen to you at all, if you are prepared to spend enough money. You can combat the wrinkles and thin hair and droopy eyelids and sagging skin and sunspots and yellowing teeth. And it appears you are expected by society to do so. And it doesn't start the day you notice that first tiny, almost invisible worry line between your brows, the faintest sunspot on your hand, a smile mark at the corner of your lips. Marketers and advertisers insist the crusade against ageing should commence no later than your teens, or even tweens.

This serves the neoliberal model very well, of course, because it means we hand over our money and drive ourselves into debt—although the more sensitive of us not unreasonably fret about where the moral line can be drawn between sensible self-care and a selfish, costly or facile obsession with appearances. A while back I read of an English businesswoman who spent $70,000 on a face lift. She said this wasn't about vanity but about 'self-respect'. To me it sounded more like fear.

The irony, as Simone de Beauvoir would have discovered had she lived in our era, is that undergoing all the latest surgeries and treatments has a surprising and perverse effect. While these adherents to cosmetic treatments don't appear to age, exactly, they don't quite look like themselves either. Take Nicole Kidman, who, aided no doubt by the best cosmetic clinicians money can buy, is impossibly smooth-cheeked, even-featured, wide-eyed and bewigged with impressive manes of hair. She still looks very beautiful, but not quite consistent with her younger self; more like a startling adult-size Nicole Kidman doll.

Meanwhile the actress Jamie Lee Curtis is widely praised for her 'courage' in daring to present herself to the world with wrinkles . . . as a healthy, happy and *ageing* woman. It seems to me a sad paradox that, even when we fervently denounce all forms of ageism as retrograde and discriminatory, and even as we applaud longevity as a social achievement, in reality we have become supremely ageist when it comes to our own bodies. We repudiate and revile our ageing human flesh. This is a particular pressure felt by women but undoubtedly and increasingly by men too. It turns ageing for all of us into a process of anxious striving, self-absorption and superficiality.

The Japanese have a cautionary tale about the fantasy of recapturing perfect youth. In the story, an elderly woodcutter and his wife are living in the woods. One day, the old man walks further than usual and comes upon a stream of sparkling water. On impulse, he kneels and drinks from the stream. When he stands up, he discovers in the water's reflection that he has become a young man again, as vigorous and handsome as he had been in his youth. Running home, he calls excitedly to his wife: 'Go to the stream and drink from it, and we shall both be young again.' The wife finds her way to the stream and begins to drink. The water is so refreshing she does not stop; she drinks and drinks. Finally, her husband becomes concerned about his wife's prolonged absence and heads back to the stream to find her. There he discovers a little baby, because his wife has drunk too greedily of the fountain of youth. There it is: the quest for eternal youth presented as an 'infantile' aspiration.

If it's a crime to look your age these days, it's just as bad to act it. Marketing directed at ageing baby boomers holds up a flattering mirror to geriatric vigour, vitality, sexuality and potency. Go on, it says, hike that Grade 4 trail and get the tattoo. Run the half-marathon, especially if it's in some exotic location that you can boast about to your friends. Leave the husband at home for a while or forever and go off backpacking with your friends. Take a lover or a third wife, if you can afford her.[1]

It's all a very long way from Cicero in his Italian vineyard, advising his fellow elders to get into the garden and explore the life of the mind; to settle into wisdom and offer support to the young.

FOUNTAINS OF YOUTH?

One of the bestselling books on how to achieve longevity is called *Outlive*. What a title: life as a competition, like the TV show *Survivor*. If you outplay and outlast everyone, you win.

And what exactly, I ask myself, do you win? Should it be my life's mission from now on to try to outrun my own death? The writer Robert M. Pirsig nailed the apparent circularity of the longevity ambition in his book *Zen and the Art of Motorcycle Maintenance*: 'One lives longer in order that one may live longer. There is no other purpose.'

I know people who have outlived their siblings, spouses and friends. It is a cruel kind of victory. When my mother was 85 years old, she received the news of the death of one of her oldest and dearest friends with compressed lips and a frozen expression. No sighs, no tears, no reminiscences. She couldn't see the point of bothering others with her long-ago memories and complex grief. But I could see in her eyes the lonely pain of her survival.

The author of *Outlive* is Dr Peter Attia.[2] At the outset, he acknowledges that if you are reading his book and you've had a heart attack or cancer or live with diabetes then you are probably not going to excel in his project. Well, with a stent in an artery in my own heart, possibly caused by side effects from chemotherapy for an aggressive 'triple negative' breast cancer, that may count me out. The statistics show that those who have been healthy over the course of their lives can expect to live longest. As well as, in all probability, being genetically fortunate, those are the same people who eat well and exercise and use their minds. Who are, in other words, reasonably well educated and well off. For those of us who have experienced heart problems or cancer or lived unwisely and too well, there is still a good chance we will enjoy longer lives if we make the right diet and exercise modifications, and Attia reassures readers that these can be surprisingly effective even if commenced later in life.

I became suspicious of Attia's analysis, however, when I realised that there was a third element to his life-enhancing agenda: anti-ageing drugs. An entire chapter is devoted to a pilgrimage made by Dr Attia and three male friends to Easter Island to marvel together at the sacred place where a rare molecule was first discovered in the 1960s. The drug created from this miraculous molecule is called rapamycin, linking it forever to the island's Indigenous name, Rapa Nui, and associating it with the romantic mysteries of the great Easter Island stone statues and the lost, heroic culture they are assumed to represent.

The Greek historian Herodotus thought the fountain of youth might be located in Ethiopia; Alexander the Great was on the lookout for it as he rampaged from Macedonia to India; Dr Attia reckons he found it on Easter Island.

Dr Attia himself is so dazzled by the properties of rapamycin that he declares in *Outlive* and, beyond that, online and in his public appearances, that he doses himself with this wonder drug. Attia admits that his ingestion is 'experimental' at this stage. The drug has not so far received FDA clearance; the official medical community does not yet recognise ageing as a disease. This is a big mistake, in Attia's opinion. In fact, an important motivation in writing *Outlive,* he says, is to 'start a conversation' about the need to understand ageing as a 'disease' that medicine can cure.

There we have it. Ageing is no longer the natural fate of every living thing, but an ugly yet curable disease. You can take this as an important new scientific insight or as the misguided quest for eternal youth dressed up in modern terms.

The ancient Greeks had a typically black and hilarious take on the subject: it's the story of the immortal goddess Eos, who falls in love with a human man, Tithonus. She asks the great god Zeus to grant Tithonus eternal life so they can be together forever. But there's a twist. Eos forgets to ask Zeus to grant Tithonus eternal youth along with eternal life, so the hapless goddess finds herself tied forever to a withered, toothless old man who cannot die. When it comes to longevity, when it comes to that dream of eternal youth, be careful what you wish for.

Attia himself is exhilarated by the prospect. He offers two contrasting graphs to illustrate the momentous change underway in the very structure and shape of human lives.

Attia shows the average present-day 'lifespan' as a horizontal line that turns into a long, slow, sad, curving decline, filled with cancer or Alzheimer's or diabetes or heart disease. He argues that it's this prolonged tail end of life that is the big problem.

He then contrasts this dismal picture with a new life measure: a 'healthspan'. This is a considerably longer horizontal line of great good health, with a short but steep decline at the end. He is convinced that a significantly shorter proportion of our long life will be spent in decline, in that frail and debilitated state so many older people endure today. If true, the implications are profound. No more mouldering in the aged care facility. No more decade-long debility caused by the modern lifestyle diseases of Alzheimer's or cancers or diabetes or heart disease. Death is deferred, and when it comes it is relatively quick and far more dignified. In theory, that is.

In practice, however, right now this is highly unlikely. The fact is that modern medicine has devised endlessly inventive new ways to further extend a miserable quality of life, as laid out with disturbing clarity in American surgeon Atul Gawande's 2014 book *Being Mortal*. As Gawande explains, 'The interval between moving to a terminal condition and actually dying has elongated massively.' Death once obediently and punctually followed a terminal diagnosis; it was a matter of days, weeks or months. Now, though, with medical interventions, we know that death can be delayed for many, many years.

In 2025, when former US president Joe Biden was diagnosed with advanced prostate cancer at the age of 83, journalists began polishing their obituaries. But those reporters were working from a now-defunct paradigm. The medical establishment jumped in to correct this outdated thinking and reminded the public that innovative cancer therapies these days meant that President Biden would receive ongoing treatment (no doubt involving pain and suffering, although they didn't mention that) but would very possibly die of something else. In other words, these days you can be dying for a very long time. Many people today are doing just that: half living, mostly dying.

Outlive argues for a muscular and interventionist approach to longevity, but there's another theory that operates on almost the opposite principle. The 'Blue Zone' approach looks back to gentle, ancient ways of living and traditional ways of doing things. It's based on five key principles. Eat more plants. Move naturally. Shift down a gear. Spend time with friends and family. Cultivate purpose and belonging.

In the TV series *Live to 100: Secrets of the Blue Zones*, host and advocate Dan Buettner journeys to some of the world's forgotten corners to admire the impressive longevity of people living—let's be honest—the same impoverished lifestyle endured by their forebears a thousand years earlier. Dan notes this himself as he watches some poor old Sardinian women labour up a near-vertical hill in their ancient town to attend mass in the gigantic church looming at the top. But he isn't sorry for them; he's exhilarated by the health benefits of medieval living. In the same enthused spirit, Dan shows us very old men extracting their own health benefits by herding sheep across hard rocky uplands on frozen mornings. In Okinawa, Dan visits a village where elderly Japanese people 'move naturally' and 'eat plants'—by which he means they bend and scrabble in the dirt outside their back doors to find a few weeds to throw into the miso soup. In Costa Rica the old women maintain their muscle mass via the ingenious stratagem of being too poor for electricity, which means that if they want to eat, they must pound the staple tortillas by hand. So good for muscles and bones. What Dan Buettner celebrates looks less like the fountain of youth, and more like the stoicism and tenacity of the old and poor.

What these Blue Zones have in common is relative poverty, meagre and unvaried diets, no electricity and no cars. Dan also emphasises the value of religious belief as an aid to longevity. He might be right, but I'm not planning to manufacture belief in a metaphysical overlord purely for the sake of my coronary health. This sceptical viewer also noted that the communities Dan visited shared a distinct lack of comfortable chairs or books or art or evidence of travel or even music beyond local folk songs. They lacked young people too; they had no doubt fled the endless boredom and lack of work, opportunity or change. Buettner observed how happy these old people seemed. He pointed to scenes of cheery communal gatherings and gummy smiles to prove these simple peasants have not a care in the world. Well, where there's no change or possibility of it, I suppose, there is likely to be less stress. I concluded, however, that I was perfectly prepared to sacrifice any number of years at the end of my life for the sake of new experiences, good food, diverse company, and an educated mind and the opportunity to use it.

By the end of the series, I was worried that Dan was going to openly recommend we all return to the Stone Age, when life was just *so good*, but thankfully he didn't. He made what seemed to me to be sensible recommendations about moving more, having friends and community, and eating a healthy diet based on fresh foods. And he didn't appear to be selling anything at all for profit.

But we are wise to be sceptical. Researcher Saul Justin Newman argues that 'the data on extreme human ageing is rotten from the inside out', winning a satirical Ig Nobel Prize in 2024 for 'making people laugh, then think'. Newman claims that in Dan Buettner's Blue Zone of Ikaria, for example, 72 per cent of those presumed centenarians were dead, missing or pension fraud cases. This certainly made some people laugh and reminded others of a 2010 incident in which Japanese officials went with a large cake to congratulate 'Tokyo's oldest man' on his 111th birthday, only to find him dead and mummifying in his bed. It turned out his 80-something daughter had been collecting her father's pension for years. Newman's work has not been published in a peer-reviewed journal, however, so his wholesale debunking of the Blue Zone claims should also be treated with caution.

There is still another path to longevity. If you are not

inclined to go down the quiet, Stone-Agey Blue Zone-lifestyle path, you can always fire up and speed along the high-tech route favoured these days by tech bros and wannabe neo-master race types.

This cohort is experimenting with treatments from stem-cell injections to ice baths to starvation diets and, yes, to Attia's rapamycin. Vampire-style, they even seek infusions of young people's blood plasma into their own bloodstreams. You can now find suppliers at specialist longevity spas in Switzerland and Antigua. The spirit of these endeavours is aggressively optimistic. There's talk of a new target age of 130 or even 150. Some aim to banish death altogether.

You may have seen reports of one of the more prominent global 'wellness entrepreneurs', a Californian named Bryan Johnson, memorable for his corpse-like pallor and the unnerving bodily hairlessness he puts on constant display. Johnson is now the subject of a weirdly riveting documentary, *Don't Die: The man who wants to live forever*. His 'Project Blueprint' involves making of himself an elite but lonely guinea pig, whose 24 hours each day are ruled by a regimen of sparse vegan eating that delivers no pleasure and leaves him hungry, a strict 8.30 pm bedtime, 130 different pills, extreme exercise, blood plasma injections 'donated' by his son, and even experimental and possibly dangerous gene-modification treatments regularly taken offshore.

Johnson proposes himself as a brave pathfinder for the rest of us ordinary mortals, implying that we should be grateful for his service to humanity, and insists that by being constantly filmed, monitored, measured and examined as he undergoes these treatments, he is contributing to everyone's health and longevity. I suppose we could be grateful. Or we could note sceptically that, with so many inputs to, and variables within, Johnson's health regime, those measurements can have negligible scientific value and therefore offer scant benefit for society.

Johnson laughs at the proposition put to him in the documentary that he is forming a cult, and indeed he sounds more like a man who has been indoctrinated into one, saying, 'I have found more relief in demoting my mind and elevating my body than I have in my entire life. All my life I was desperate to be free from myself.'

He may not be starting a cult but Johnson is certainly running a business. His online *Blueprint Protocol Starter Guide* issues dozens of suggestions for his eager followers, from 'grounding' bedsheets (no, I have no idea what they are either) to light therapy and blood glucose measuring devices, all of which you can buy when you click through to the recommended providers. Johnson may succeed in living forever, but the very thought of sharing endless life on earth with the likes of him is enough to make me long for the final exit.

By now you won't be surprised to hear that Johnson's longevity agenda has support at the very highest level of the Trump administration, in the form of that well-known health crank and vaccine denier Robert F. Kennedy Jr, who is currently Trump's Secretary of Health and Human Services and longevity cheerleader-in-chief. RFK Jr is here to back the president's inspiring MAGA agenda, which not only aims to help the rich get richer but help them live longer too.

In May 2025, RFK Jr caught up with podcaster Gary Brecka on *The Ultimate Human* podcast. (The name of the podcast says a lot about the repellent mentality at work here.) Brecka, a self-styled human biologist, biohacker, anti-ageing and longevity expert, boasted to his followers that his and RFK Jr's families had just returned from some hyperbaric oxygen chamber action combined with doses of nutritional IVs, and were now relaxing at Gary's place in Miami.

In their 40-minute discussion, interspersed with ads for Brecka's H2Tabs and BiOptimizers and other obscure marvels, RFK Jr assured a delighted Brecka that he was going to end the United States Food and Drug Administration's 'war' against experimental anti-ageing drugs and treatments, and thereby liberate people to use *untested drugs*.

Sure, RFK Jr said with a shrug, the FDA should continue to play a role telling the public what they've learned about drugs, but it should not tell the public what they can and can't do, nor tell physicians what they can and cannot prescribe. 'If you want to take an experimental drug,' he said, 'you can do that, *you ought to be able to do that*. You shouldn't have to go to Antigua to get stem cells.' He added, 'We don't want to have the Wild West and want to make sure the information is out there. But we also want to respect the intelligence of the American people.' (I couldn't help thinking dubiously that these would be the same American people who had voted Donald Trump in as president for a second time.) Sure, RFK Jr conceded, 'You are going to get a lot of charlatans, and people that get bad results, but ultimately you can't prevent that either way.'

Gary Brecka concluded by thanking God for RFK Jr, but now they had to wrap up because they were heading out to join President Trump at the UFC fights. Two privileged men obsessed by their own enduring potency getting thrills out of the spectacle of working people beating the daylights out of each other. With a plan to enable 'ultimate humans', people like them, to hold on to life and power forever.

Australia has so far avoided this kind of excess, I am relieved to note. But we have produced one of the more interesting examples of longevity ambition in the curious case of Rupert Murdoch. In 2023, the then 92-year-old

Murdoch announced his impending fifth marriage and presented his 66-year-old fiancée with a gigantic diamond ring. Rupert said that he and his new love were 'looking forward to the second half of our lives together'. I'm no mathematician, but Rupert seemed to be suggesting that he expected to live to 180. Increasingly fickle in what we would once have called his sunset years, Rupert soon broke off that engagement and quickly found a new 60-something partner, who in June 2024 became the fifth Mrs Murdoch.

More recently, Rupert Murdoch appears to have renounced physical longevity as his ultimate goal. Accepting the possibility that his mortal body may give up one day, he's not letting that get in the way of his quest for immortal power. Which is why he directed teams of lawyers to change the terms of the Murdoch family trust to privilege his same-mindedly conservative eldest son Lachlan over his more progressive siblings, extending Rupert's control of NewsCorp well beyond the grave. One court case to that end spectacularly failed, but a 'settlement' has now been reached that enthrones Lachlan and thereby maximises his father's goal of ideological longevity. Rupert Murdoch aims to go on forever, haunting us, dead or alive—because if you outplay and outlive, you win.

SCIENCE LEADS THE WAY

We may debate the veracity or merit of various obscure, folkish, heroic or plain fraudulent modern recipes for longevity, but what we know for certain is that science-based approaches have delivered dramatically improved health outcomes and increased longevity across the world; they continue to drive longevity outcomes today and will impose longer lives upon us in future.

Australia's leadership in the longevity mission comes indirectly from our long run of peace, prosperity and broad economic parity and directly via our strong public health system, good hospitals and implementation of advances in medical science. I note here that this health record is not equal across Australia: it includes a glaring disparity between the major advances in health and longevity for the majority and very poor health outcomes for Australia's First Nations peoples. But overall, it is impressive. It has its origins in policies created for an expanding post-war Australia. In 1965, when my baby brother was born in Mona Vale Hospital in New South Wales, a government agency filmed my smiling mother leaving the hospital with Justin in her arms. The aim was to promote Australia's widespread mother and baby health programs. These were put in place to support our post-war baby boom and greatly contributed to maternal and infant survival and health. Growing up in the sixties and seventies, there was a small glass bottle of milk left in a crate outside the school classroom every morning for each kid, rich or poor, and we were ordered to drink it for our health; the memory of that nauseatingly sun-warmed milk in summer has stayed with me to this day. Infant, childhood and teenage inoculations were mandatory and free: you'd turn up at school and find yourself getting another jab to save you and the community from some disease you'd never heard of, like tuberculosis, polio, measles and mumps, tetanus, polio or diphtheria. The consequent declines in child and infant mortality have given a permanent boost to our national longevity statistics. When Justin and I were about nine and eleven years old respectively, the Whitlam government installed sewerage in my outer Sydney suburb.

It was a massive sanitation improvement, part of the modern first-world infrastructure that has broadly eradicated diarrhoea-related disease and death.

Social engineering has also changed our society for the better to promote both safety and longevity. I grew up in the days when cars were instruments of both liberty and death. Drink driving was normal. Two uncles of mine died in road accidents. In high school everyone knew of someone's brother or cousin and their teenage mates who had fatally rammed the driver's dad's car into a telegraph pole on a night out. Drink-driving laws were transformational for everyone on the road. Mandatory seatbelts and enforced car design modifications meant fewer fatal injuries in the case of accidents. This wholesale reform process wasn't just about government innovation, by the way; the trade union movement led the way in Australia on workplace safety reforms, and today safer work practices mean far fewer fatalities and injuries at work. Governments began to run the public health campaigns that are a big part of the national health story. The 'Slip Slop Slap' sunblock promotions made major inroads into the shocking rates of skin cancer—although the appeal of sun worship is so strong in this country that this is one campaign that probably needs to be renewed for each generation. Anti-cigarette smoking campaigns markedly reduced the incidence of lung cancer deaths and changed our culture, or at least until the current vaping scourge. The HIV/AIDS campaigns were groundbreaking and effective in promoting safe sex behaviours and reducing transmission through shared needles by intravenous drug users.

When I was growing up, a diagnosis of cancer was almost always a death sentence, or so it seemed. Two of my aunts died of breast cancer. Many great-uncles died slowly or quickly of skin or lung or liver cancer. Not today. Preventive measures such as those campaigns against smoking or sun exposure or alcohol consumption have had a hugely beneficial impact on the cancer numbers. Beyond this, early detection rates, achieved through regular screenings for breast, cervical and bowel cancers, have made it easier to treat disease before it spreads. When cancer is diagnosed, the blunt instruments of surgery, radiation and chemotherapy are still being deployed, but with more sophistication to increase survival rates, minimise suffering and enhance quality of life. (I say 'minimise', but that is a euphemism. Any woman who has endured the horrible side effects of breast cancer chemotherapy is shocked that she has survived the cure, let alone the disease.)

In the near future, treatments will be targeted more precisely to the biology of each patient. Scientists are already able to look at the composition and behaviour of cancer cells taken from an individual and grown in real time. New 'precision medicines' will be targeted to each individual's genetic make-up. One of these rapidly developing therapies involves utilising a patient's own immune system to fight cancer, a major breakthrough. For people living in First World countries, these developments are likely to mean the end of cancer as a death sentence.

Genetic diseases, affecting children, are diverse and rare in themselves, but together they contribute to a great deal of early death and disease. With the cost of DNA testing going down rapidly, scientists now have increasing access to information-rich genetic data banks that will help them to identify which populations, which families and even which individuals are at risk of a wide range of genetically induced cancers, heart disease and auto-immune diseases. Gene-editing technologies are still in their early days but it's clear that sooner rather than later scientists will be able to edit out disease-causing genetic material in living patients. This will have massive implications for curing genetic disease in individuals but also for the eradication of hereditary diseases altogether.

For most of human history, epidemics caused by viruses, parasites and bacteria have periodically depleted entire populations. Our thorough vaccination regimes today help us to avoid most of them. The COVID-19 experience showed us that while terrible global epidemics are still possible, and globalisation means disease can spread faster and further than ever (especially via aircraft and cruise ships), we'll have the means to cope. That's not to say COVID-19 didn't have a short-term effect: Australian life expectancy actually fell slightly in 2022. But COVID-19 also fast-tracked the introduction of an important new vaccine therapy that uses genetic code to tell the human body how to manage the virus by itself. It's the beginning of a new wave of therapies, making it more likely—if the current US administration doesn't destroy all its medical research capability—that future pandemics will have no more than a temporary impact on overall longevity trends.

So, I hear you ask, perhaps even plaintively, with clever and dedicated humans having prevented or eradicated or mitigated so many sources of disease and injury, *what on earth will we have left to kill us?* Well, we do still have a few major killers—on paper, at least. They still include cancers of various kinds, especially lung cancer. But even if you die from cancer one day, it will still take far, far longer than it would have in the past. You can be kept alive for a very long time, so long as you are prepared to tolerate the excruciating 'mix and match' of surgery, chemotherapy, radiation and medication, plus some of the new auto-immune therapies. And not only once each, but potentially over and over again.

Then there are the various vascular diseases—including heart attacks, heart disease and strokes—caused by cellular waste and fatty build-ups clogging our blood vessels: they might still finish you off. Eventually. After a long time. Again, however, a modern management regime, including surgery and medication, is very good at extending lives. I have had two operations to wedge open my 90 per cent-clogged left arterial descending artery (the first attempt was an experimental model that failed). I was awake both times, in no pain, and the benefits were immediate. Practical diet and exercise programs as mandated by doctors in the follow-up can dramatically improve outcomes. For those whose heart has totally failed, the last-ditch option is for someone else to die and pass on their hand-me-down heart, with all the attendant risks of bodily rejection. Now even that's changing: Australia is leading the world on the creation of artificial hearts that will soon, probably, be available and effective. The advances keep advancing, and so does our life span.

Then there is dementia. That's different. In its various forms, dementia is the worst fate of all: cruellest for the sufferer and traumatic and devastating for their families, as a fully formed human being loses aspects of their memory and identity and sometimes becomes almost unrecognisable to themselves and to those who know them best. The likelihood of developing dementia increases significantly with age. In Australia today, according to the Commonwealth Department of Health website, you'll see that one in twelve people aged 65 and over is living with dementia. One in twelve. There is still no cure for dementia and, as far as I know, no cure is imminent. With all the other diseases under much better control, dementia has now taken over from coronary heart disease as the leading cause of death in Australia. That's a slightly misleading statistic, however. The bigger problem with dementia is that it kills its victims slowly.

These major diseases—cancer, heart disease and stroke, and to some extent dementia—are often described as diseases of 'lifestyle', by which the experts mean poor diet, alcohol abuse, cigarette smoking, stress and lack of exercise. Today we have a fresh batch of lifestyle diseases to mull over. Experts are concerned about the health and longevity prospects for children brought up on processed foods, junk treats, chemical drinks and giant meal portions, who lack exercise and free play, and suffer depression and anxiety made worse by an overload of toxic screen time—not to mention the cancer-causing properties of nanoparticles and microplastics, the impact of climate change broadly and the effects on our health of extreme weather.

There's another proximate cause of First World death that anyone with an aged relative will be aware of by now: death by falls. According to the Australian Bureau of Statistics, accidental falls were the eleventh biggest cause of death in Australia in 2022, up from eighteenth ten years earlier. Both my parents died in hospital following falls in their aged care home. It's particularly lethal to older people due to their porous, brittle, so-easily-breakable bones and the downstream complications that can result from the traumatic injuries.

This will remain a problem for the near future but will likely be less of an issue in the long term. Attention is now being directed to helping people maintain bone health and good balance into old age. Targeted balance, stability and weight-lifting programs, especially aimed at older women, are being trialled, and the evidence so far is that the loss of bone mass can be stalled, and bone mass may even build back to some extent.

I am one of those weight-lifting women. After a year in the program, I can report that the decline in my bone mass has stabilised and my strength and balance have significantly improved. My observation and experience is that those of us taking these classes feel more physically and psychologically confident about dealing with the ageing process.

But if health and well-being can be prolonged by good habits, when poor health finally arrives it won't necessarily, or even probably, shorten life's suffering.

An American Medical Association report published in 2024 reveals that Australia is in the forefront, just fractionally behind the USA, in the number of years people are living with chronic disease. As Professor Stephen Simpson, an eminent biological scientist and co-author of the groundbreaking book *Eat Like the Animals*, told me, 'The combination of an advanced healthcare system with an industrialised food system is the (slow) killer. We are rich enough to kill ourselves slowly.' Australians on average now spend more than twelve years at the end of their long lives in poor health, according to research into the 'healthspan-lifespan gap' conducted by two Mayo Clinic researchers. Think about that: twelve long, long years.

What we are seeing now and can expect to see well into the future is that we will have large numbers of Australians with various co-morbidities who will nevertheless be kept 'alive' with a poor quality of life—and we are expected to hail this as a great achievement.

Longevity is not, of course, simply or even mainly a matter for individuals and families. It is changing the very shape and structure of our society. As the proportion of older people grows, the proportion of young people and children shrinks. This trend is magnified because Australian women are giving up on having children. Australian women are now predicted to have an average of 1.6 babies between 2024 and 2029, well below the international average of 2.3 and a near record low birth rate for Australia.

I have now heard two treasurers in my lifetime begging the women of Australia to have children. The first was

Liberal treasurer Peter Costello, who urged us to have 'one for yourself, one for your husband and one for the country': that didn't go down well. And then there was Labor treasurer Jim Chalmers, father of three, saying much the same thing in 2024 during a cost-of-living and home ownership and accommodation crisis. His message was greeted with barely muffled guffaws.

One reason why governments are so keen to have more young people around the place is because they will be needed to pay the taxes and do the labour to care for so many old Australians. Remember that 40 per cent of additional future expenditure in the 2023 Intergenerational Report? And if we think there is a problem today with a bulge of older Australians, then get ready . . .

The key metric is the old-age to working-age ratio. This is the number of people aged 65 and over for every 100 people of traditional working age. It relies on three things: mortality rates, fertility rates and in or outflows of migration. In Australia it is currently projected to climb to the point where, by 2063, there will only be five working-age Australians for every two older people. That is an entirely confronting notion, and it's even worse than you'd think, because a 'working-age' Australian is still defined as anyone aged between 15 and 64. Do you know any fifteen-year-old earning a living and paying tax? Me neither. If current government policy ambitions are fulfilled, a full 80 per cent of young Australians will be leaving school only to enter some form of tertiary education. That pushes the working-age start time back even further. Meanwhile, aged care costs will just go up and up to meet the needs of ageing baby boomers. Imagine how young working people will feel when they discover just how much of their tax payment is devoted to propping up the lives of very old people.

When it comes to addressing this very real national challenge, once again we confront our national inability to imagine and build a society in which it is in the clear interests of women to have children. It is as if Australian men and women live in two different countries. The men live in a dynamic economy, thinking about options for themselves in careers, housing and lifestyle. But women, even if they are encouraged to *Aim high!* and *Chase your dreams!* while they are girls and teenagers, are somehow expected to revert in their twenties and thirties to a state of premodern saintliness, immune to these individualist aspirations and selfish modern wants, happy to sacrifice their personal fulfilment as, each night, they tuck a child, maybe two, into bed, guiltily ring their aged parents to make sure they are still alive, before they head back to the computer for another two hours of work. I know more than a few mothers who would have *loved* to have had more children but felt they simply could not manage the financial burden, not to mention the domestic labour. That seems to me to be a societal failure.

Now, I've noticed that those who preach the wonders of the new longevity are mostly men, and—permit me a crude generalisation here—men are not necessarily best placed to understand what the emerging familial and social construct, where old people live on and dominate while young people are in short supply and lack power, will mean in everyday life.

The real bedtime story is that women are supposed to produce children for the sake of an economy in which they remain second-class citizens in terms of power, opportunity and income, including when it comes to their own retirement years. Meanwhile, the glorious long-lived future for the Australian nation as it currently stands will depend not only on our individual efforts to stay fit and well but also on an army of carers for the large and small needs of ageing Australians.

The myth is that we will all be living in our homes till we drop dead, with our children and perhaps subsidised care workers popping in and helping us out when we need it. The reality, as Atul Gawande notes, is that, 'As fewer of us are struck dead out of the blue, most of us will spend significant periods of our lives too reduced and debilitated to live independently.'

A more realistic expectation for this stage of life is that

we will shuffle passively or resentfully in large numbers into aged care to be looked after by relatively low-paid workers imported into Australia from Nepal and elsewhere. This will give us a bigger national economy, but not necessarily a richer society. For one thing, it will exacerbate competition for housing as those workers who settle in Australia will eventually have their own small Australian-sized families and, as they age, they will need carers too. It's a population Ponzi scheme that will put more pressure on Australia's fragile ecology and make it harder than ever for us to meet our climate change targets.

Meanwhile, I do hear occasional cheering tales of medical professionals who still fly the rebel flag for pleasure, for a life that is worth living for as long as possible. A friend of mine has two doctors: one is an Australian puritan living in Sydney and the other is a French bon viveur living in Beijing. The Australian doctor ordered my friend to exercise vigorously and abandon many of the things he most enjoyed in life, including red wine and camembert. My friend wisely sought a second opinion from his French doctor, who considered this dour advice and then offered a more balanced view of the health imperative: *You must live a little, eh? Maybe just limit the wine to one bottle a night instead of two.*

A COMPLETED LIFE

It's the 21st century and we are still pretending that if you die peacefully and painlessly in a bed at a ripe old age it's a matter of tremendous shock and upset. In this era of longevity, we need new ways to think, talk, plan and act around death. Sensible ways. And really, why wouldn't we do this? We are no longer a society led by a caste of all-powerful priests like the Christian clergy who kept our forebears in a state of fearful terror about death, and even more terrified of what might come after.

Australians who don't want to live in a suffering, dependent state, who want to live with autonomy and die with it too, will need to argue for it. We will need to demand more information about our health options and more choice about the timing and manner of our own deaths. There will be resistance to this. For the private medical sector there is big money to be made off the long-living bodies of patients: dead bodies are good for nothing but the grave and the furnace. And there will always be people with religious convictions seeking to impose their views on us.

Victorian literature from Charles Dickens to Thomas Hardy and Elizabeth Gaskell reeks with morally redeeming scenes of deathbed suffering, and the consolations afforded not only to the soon-to-be-dead but also to those who witnessed the patient's agony and were schooled by it in the virtues of faith and fortitude. At that time, before the advent of quality pain relief, even Victorian medical practitioners cheerfully deferred to the priests as a source of authority for the stricken and dying.

In her 2023 book *The Good Death Through Time*, historian Caitlin Mahar vividly portrayed the Victorian clergyman's dominant role beside the household deathbed, extracting that one final abject confession from the poor scared human hoping to float gently up to Heaven rather than be flung down by God to Hell. She quoted the ghoulish Dr Samuel Beckett, who observed in 1854 that it was better to die awake and in slow agony from consumption than in the blur of fever or a sudden accident. It was, he wrote, 'delightful to witness the calm, heavenly and truly edifying bearing and conversation of a pious young person slowly wearing away under pulmonary consumption'.[3]

Today, your time of death and mine is no longer in the hands of the gods; it's the doctors who are firmly in charge of our dying process. Given the many new and experimental medical options available, patients—including old ones—are routinely being offered treatment after treatment by medical professionals who are more worried about their medico-legal risks than your comfort or wishes. They may tell themselves they are extending life when in effect they are often protracting the dying process.

And while you might think that medical doctors would be the last people in the world to take their interpersonal communication cues from the mystical blather of the clergy, it's my experience that the modern medical profession seems equally averse to honest talk about grave illness and imminent death. They just do the mumbo-jumbo a bit differently.

As a result, there's an oddly euphemistic pseudo-medical language that all children of elderly parents must learn to decipher (or be taught by exhausted friends who have already been through the experience) if they are to have any hope of staying sane while managing the final phase of a parent's life. It goes like this . . . You find yourself in emergency with your much-loved parent who is very old, terribly frail and clearly gravely injured after their bad fall, and to your amazement the doctors seem quite determined *not* to recognise the obvious fact, which is that they are going to die. In my mother Clare's case, I made the supreme error of asking the doctor straight out if that was the case. He winced, and I felt like the pleb lowering the tone at an upper-class English dinner party. Instead, in a corrective tone of voice, with a lowered chin, he said that her fall was indeed 'an end-of-life event'. Right. Got it.

When Dad was lying on the hospital bed after his big fall, sedated but still clearly in pain, I had fortunately been forewarned that I needed to tell the doctors that 'his comfort' should be their priority. Yes, euphemisms in a modern hospital. *Dad's comfort is the priority*, I found myself repeating with stagey exaggeration. I did not actually wink, but the brief knowing nod I received in reply was a return sign that the code had worked. They would not have been at all okay with upping the morphine level so that Dad died in painless bliss—but they were absolutely fine with providing extensive 'comfort measures' which turned out to mean doing exactly that.

Once you've all finally agreed that the dying person is, in fact, going to die, it gets even more bewildering, because the hospital doesn't really want to know you. I can say from experience that the dying person is moved to the equivalent of the spare room out the back. Probably with a broken window and some leftover equipment. The morphine is briskly organised, and the family is left to watch and wait over their dying. I presume the hospital doesn't really want to know you because these clinicians are, after all, in the beautiful life-at-any-price business, not the unseemly, ill-paid, statistically unhelpful death business. Which is deeply ironic given, as Haider Warraich writes in his book *Modern Death*, 'To a great extent, both ordinary people and the medical community have accepted practices very close to, if not indistinguishable from, euthanasia.'[4]

In *Being Mortal*, Dr Atul Gawande steps back from the end-of-life crisis to portray a broader United States medical culture in which clinicians are reluctant to engage realistically with their patients throughout the course of their relationship, reluctant to correct their patients' misguided hopes of a miracle, reluctant to admit their cancers are not curable. The clinician too often takes the easy path and offers the terminally ill patient treatment after treatment that may marginally prolong their life but simultaneously cause great suffering, potentially wasting the precious time that patient has left.

According to Gawande, even when pressed by their patients for the truth about their circumstances, clinicians resist saying plainly what lies ahead. This failure of honest talking has serious implications for the patient and for the medical system. According to Gawande, studies showed more than 40 per cent of oncologists admitted to prescribing treatments they believed were unlikely to work.

This is a medical model where ethical failure and moral cowardice meet economic self-interest. There's money to be made in all those pointless procedures. But for the patient, as Gawande notes, 'People die only once. They have no experience to draw on. They need doctors and nurses who are willing to have the hard discussions and say what they have seen, who will help people prepare for what is to come.' Gawande says out loud what I have heard no other doctor admit, which is that this approach inflicts 'new forms of physical torture' on both the elderly and those with terminal illnesses.

We have the same problem here. We see doctors unwilling to tell their patients that they've run out of viable medical options for their conditions. Instead, they will 'helpfully' propose more rounds of chemo, that tricky operation, the new experimental treatment. The risks of terrible side effects from such treatments or operations, sometimes life-threatening ones, may be mentioned (as legally required), but only in passing and often underplayed. So is the likelihood that the treatment may only offer temporary relief. No doubt it is all too easy, as a clinician, to persuade yourself that you are doing the right thing when, if your patient is still earnestly looking for a longer life, less pain or more mobility, they agree to a risky or inappropriate course of action.

In 2019, a 60-plus man died in a regional Australian private hospital from a heart attack brought on by a pulmonary thromboembolism, just three days after his orthopaedic surgeon ill-advisedly replaced both knees in the one aggressive operation. The inquest was told that this man had an extensive list of health issues, including coronary artery disease. Under questioning about the patient's fitness for such high-stress surgery, the anaesthetist merely noted, among other things, that 'he was very keen' to have it.

The 'customer is always right' approach to modern medicine is surely wrong. But counterproductive or minimally effective medical overservicing for the old or seriously ill should not be ascribed only or even mainly to greed, cowardice or laziness. Much of it no doubt relates to the ancient code of honour and the societal prestige that medical doctors still attach to the Hippocratic commitment to 'do no harm'. If death is the ultimate harm, then life and life only must be the indubitable measure of professional and ethical success. Their commitment to that oath is why doctors will agree to try anything to keep you or your loved ones alive for just that little bit longer. At all costs. At any price.

In aid of a more rational and enlightened approach, Atul Gawande has proposed a reframing of the medical mission away from a crusade against death and towards helping people 'live well and die well' too. Gawande founded Ariadne Labs in Boston in 2012 for this very purpose: to train clinicians to have more honest and compassionate conversations with their elderly and gravely ill patients about what is happening to them, so the patients might have 'more, better, and earlier conversations with their clinicians about their goals, values, and priorities that will inform their future care'. It doesn't surprise me that the feedback so far shows that plain-speaking conversations lead to *less* anxiety and depression. And healthcare costs are reduced for the community as patients are steered away from pointless, painful treatments and towards the fulfilment of their own end-of-life wishes.

In Australia we now have voluntary euthanasia laws in all states and territories (except the Northern Territory), whereby eligible adults with a terminal illness may ask for and obtain help from a health practitioner to end their life. These laws vary slightly but, with the exception of the Australian Capital Territory, they have two things in common: the individual must have a life expectancy of no more than six months (twelve in Tasmania if they have a neurodegenerative disease) and they must be able to provide informed consent at every stage. Unlike the other jurisdictions, the ACT's scheme, which came into effect in late 2025, does not require someone to have a diagnosed 'timeframe' until death. This promises a more sensible and compassionate system, but it's too soon to tell.

Modest as our laws are, they are still controversial in other jurisdictions. In 2025 I followed the debate as the British Parliament considered a bill along the lines of the Australian model, allowing terminally ill adults with six months or less to live to get medical assistance to end their own lives. The result, as one advocate of the change reminded the Parliament, would be that 'no more people will die but far fewer people will suffer'.

It was enlightening to witness the vehement opposition to this restrained piece of legislation on the part of some lawmakers and members of the medical profession. One insisted this would break the 'sacred bond of trust between doctor and patient'. Another claimed, 'One person's right to die will become another person's duty to die. If it becomes law, then [the attitude will be] *it must be right* and that is *not good for civilisation.*'

But how is it good for 'civilisation' to condemn citizens to unnecessary suffering and misery before they die when they have the tools to alleviate that pain?

Atul Gawande's holistic medical agenda openly addresses the concerns of those clinicians who fear that helping their patients to die will implicate them in unbecoming death/failure scenarios and remove their hallowed association with life/health/success. His program includes the training of more specialist geriatricians who can promote longer and better health for older people, plus investment in quality palliative care at home or in hospices to help the mortally ill die in comfort.

As I understand it, Gawande does not himself support voluntary assisted dying, but I see his pragmatic and compassionate mantra—that the task of modern medicine should be to help patients 'to live well and die well'—as an ethical framework suitable for modern Australia. This approach, which is beginning to emerge here, will reduce the economic burden on the insanely overstretched hospital system, prevent the rampant overservicing of patients that occurs today, and deliver happier and more peaceful deaths for patients and less trauma for families. But implementing these improvements takes time; those specialist skills in geriatrics and the facilities for palliative care can't be conjured up overnight.

In the meantime, for those of us who are patients, the primary tool we have at our disposal to ensure our wishes are respected in case of grave illness is our Advance Care Directive. These are a good idea in principle. In practice, no one in a hospital emergency setting ever asked me or my brother whether there was an ACD for either of our parents. That was particularly odd given that each of them had arrived at hospital from their aged care facility. One of the conclusions of the 2021 Royal Commission into Aged Care Quality and Safety was that aged care facilities need to do more to support the use of Advance Care Directives, but the relevant legislation only came into effect in November 2025. We'll see how that works, and if it improves hospital procedures.

Advance Care Directives are important, but even if taken into consideration they have their limitations. In filling out my own ACD I designated my husband as my 'person responsible' in the event, as the form puts it, that 'I am not able to understand and make decisions about my treatment or can't tell the doctors or my family'. My husband and I have had discussions about my preferences, and I have no doubt he'll respect them, sensible man, but others may not be so lucky.

In *Modern Death*, which focuses on the American experience, Warraich reveals how often conflicts arise at a patient's end of life—not because the patient's expressed wishes represent a problem to the clinicians, but because family members decide to override them. Warraich noted that surrogates 'deviate frequently from their stated roles and often make judgments based on their own values and with interests in mind other than the patient's. One told the doctor, "She always said she wouldn't want to live on a machine but right now I'm making the decision that it's best for her to be on the machine."'

I looked up the reviews of *Modern Death* on Goodreads. One reader, who described herself as a nurse, reported her own bleak experience liaising with families who would not accept that their loved one should be helped to die gently, in line with their own wishes. She described how hard it was to be asked by families and doctors to participate in 'medical battery on the elderly' with 'torturous procedures, tests, and invasions thrust upon the dying'.

For my part, I would also want this understood: what good does it serve me to be kept alive in continuous pain or disability or loss of selfhood except to diminish my good life by a sad, unnecessarily elongated death? Personally, I don't need to live to 100. In fact, if I start losing my wits, or life after 75 is too painful and unpleasant, I'd like to be able to end it myself painlessly or authorise some person or mechanism to kindly end it for me. I would support this approach because I cannot forget that awful statistic: Australia is at the global forefront with the cruel achievement of giving its citizens twelve years of suffering with chronic disease.

I think there will be some, perhaps many, like me who have been through tough medical treatments over the course of their life, feel that they have physically and psychologically suffered enough medical interventions to stay alive for their own sake and for their families, and at a decent age want to have some control over their own dying. We are moderns, are we not? We live every day with freedom, risk and choice. We are expected to take responsibility for ourselves throughout our lives. Yet when it comes to our death, we are abruptly rendered powerless. What is the worst that can happen? A peaceful autonomous death a few months or years earlier than the suffering and drawn-out death that would otherwise occur? That's hardly a tragedy; that's what we used to call a blessing.

And when I am 80-something, I don't want to hear that, in making such a request, I could only be doing it 'under pressure'. Surely it isn't wrong for me to prefer *not* to be remembered as sad, silent, demented or incontinent. I don't think it's wrong to take into account the needs and interests of those who love me and whom I love, who would otherwise have to bear the long stressful burden of caring for me, who might benefit from any inheritance I will leave, and who may otherwise be left with traumatic memories of my end days. And if I am alone and poor and sad, who is to say that I shouldn't have the right to ease my own suffering and conclude my life on my own terms?

I'm no sovereign individual adrift on my personal island. Consideration for society is part of my humanity and my intergenerational duty. If I felt that I were ready for my life to end, and satisfied that my life was complete,

I would be pleased to take care of my own end-of-life, take some small burden off the health system and give way for younger Australians.

In the Netherlands a public discussion is under way about this very issue. In November 2023, the Dutch political party D66 drafted a bill to give people aged 75 and over the option to have euthanasia if they felt they had 'completed' life. A survey found a massive 80 per cent of voters believed that people should be able to seek help in dying when they feel they've come to the end of their life. Only 10 per cent of respondents disagreed with the statement that people who consider their lives complete should be able to end their lives with professional help. The other 10 per cent of voters had no opinion on the matter.

For many, this kind of talk, however carefully framed, raises the spectre of a society readying itself to sacrifice its sick and aged. In response, I point to the devastating rebuttal put forward by Gawande himself: 'What if the sick and aged are *already* being sacrificed—victims of our refusal to accept the inexorability of our life cycle?'

Professor Michael Cholbi, founder of the International Association for the Philosophy of Death and Dying, further tested this line of thinking: 'If assisted suicide represents a hubristic attempt to usurp nature and replace it with human judgment, then why is it not equally hubristic to try to delay death through medical means. . .?'[5]

There are still those who think that 'premature' or 'unnatural' death represents a denial of some potentially beautiful insight or spiritual end-of-life experience. On this, two case studies are worth consideration. Daniel Kahneman died on 27 March 2024. He had been a Nobel Prize-winning pioneer in the field of behavioural economics; author of *Thinking, Fast and Slow*, a groundbreaking analysis of human decision-making. One of his many insights concerned the way we humans look back at our experiences and judge them in hindsight. He coined the term 'peak-end rule', arguing that our final assessment of a life event like a marriage or a job, whether we think of it as having been good or bad, is heavily based on the experience at its peak, but also the success or otherwise of its *conclusion*. The end matters. And he acted on his own insight. Kahneman had nursed his wife through her final years with dementia and seen what a terrible final chapter that can be. Before his own death, Kahneman wrote a final email to his friends: 'I have believed that the miseries and indignities of the last years of life are superfluous, and I am acting on that belief.' Then he flew to Switzerland, aged 90 and in comparatively good health, and died calmly of his own volition at an assisted suicide centre.

Compare that outcome with Pope Francis's demise about a year later. This gentle man was peacefully nearing the end of his life in the hands of his doctors in April 2025 when his dedicated nurse openly defied God or nature and insisted the doctors use their medical expertise to keep the Holy Father alive. Due to this gross intervention, the poor fellow recovered sufficiently for a bumpy ride in his Popemobile through St Peter's Square . . . only to attend a meet-up with JD Vance, vice-president to Donald Trump. At the photo session, the look of horror on Francis's face says it all; it's as if he has already found himself in hell. Pope Francis expired soon after, his will to live surely fatally weakened by the encounter. And I doubt that, in his dying moments, he felt grateful to his nurse for those extra few days.

In the end, of course, it's up to our medical professionals to work with us, to acknowledge and take proper responsibility for what they now control, which is the whole life and death ride. In her 2019 book *A Better Death*, Australian doctor and author Ranjana Srivastava critiques current Australian medical culture, whereby Australian doctors avoid honest conversations with their patients. 'If we want to do our best,' she says, addressing her peers directly, 'we must be bold enough to broach the subject of dying'.[6]

This means being ready to adopt a compassionate whole-of-life approach to serving patients; talking openly with older patients about their wishes concerning their medical care; helping them to understand and complete their Advance Care Directive, if necessary; and, most of all, ensuring their wishes are accessible when needed by urging or arranging to help them upload their ACD to their My Health Record. This is particularly important for people from non-English-speaking backgrounds.

Clinicians in emergency departments should equally be required and empowered to seek out these directives and fully respect the wishes expressed—and, if necessary, to ignore the well-meaning but wrong-headed wishes of the family.

I think doctors might be surprised what they discover if they really listen to their patients. As Atul Gawande notes, 'It is not death that the very old tell me they fear. It is what happens short of death—losing their hearing, their memory, their best friends, their way of life.'

Today there will be people who don't want to live at all costs, for they have lived long enough. They feel their life to be whole, resolved, completed. They are ready to end it in an orderly self-directed way—and ready to hand over to the next generation.

LONGEVITY'S VICTIMS

Looked at one way, the modern longevity narrative is an inspirational story of human scientific and social progress. Looked at another, you could say that we are now condemned to longevity—our own and other people's. It's placing a massive economic, social and psychological burden on us as individuals and as a society.

There are now so many old people that new categories of demographic definition have been created to describe them. Those considered the 'young old' are aged between 55 and 65. That's me: at 63 years of age, I'm a young old. By all the rules of human history, I should have been dead for years. Instead, when I look twenty years into the future, I foresee an even older me who will need to plan for the real possibility that I may have another twenty years to go. This is not necessarily, in my view, a glorious prospect.

The 'middle old' is the cohort of people aged between 65 and 85. As the 2023 Intergenerational Report tells us, by 2063 almost a quarter of Australians will be aged between 65 and 85, more than double their number today. Consider that: around one in four. People aged 85 and over today are now described as the 'old old'. There will be more and more of those super oldies: by 2063 there will be three times as many of them as there are today. And finally, the Intergenerational Report also tells us that the cohort of centenarians will be *six times* larger than today. You will probably be alive when this demographic revolution occurs, and if things go on like this, I may be too.

In 2014, Harvard University scientist and longevity expert David Sinclair described the joys of longevity to an eager audience at the University of New South Wales, among them a friend of mine. Sinclair painted a heartwarming portrait of multiple generations of healthy active older people living their best lives. He urged the audience to consider the joy and happiness when not two, not three, not four, not five, but *six* generations of your family were brought together every Christmas and feast day.

My friend's initial reaction to this expert's forecast was the same as mine: anyone who thinks a family gathering is automatically going to be a happy affair is a fool; presuming that even bigger family gatherings are automatically going to be even happier is simply insane. For a start, who these days has a dining table that big? It was fair to assume, we agreed, that this eminent scientist had never been the poor sap expected to host and cater for extended family events. That job generally falls, as we know, to a woman, to women, who still carry so much of the emotional and practical load in family life.

And let us imagine what this multi-multi-generational family event might look like. Until very recently, the elders in a large family were a small minority: the grandparents and great-aunts seated in the comfy chairs with the younger generations spilling out noisily around them. As the birth-rate continues to decline, however, the old will loom disproportionately large and the young will be represented at family gatherings in ever smaller and lonelier proportions.

I can't bring myself to compute Sinclair's six generations, and frankly the maths is beyond me, but let me dare to contemplate the impact of 'just' four generations on family gatherings. We're heading there already. With the rise of single-child families, and the increase in longevity, it's not unlikely that we will see more cases of eight living great-grandparents per one child. How would that solitary child feel at the family event? No siblings or cousins to muck about with. No renegade uncles and wicked aunts to lighten the atmosphere. Something like this is already happening in places like China and Japan. I suspect the children at the bottom of this generational pile will feel unbearably lonely, not to mention oppressed by their looming care duties for all those elders.

Now imagine that poor woman doing the hosting and catering duties for these events. She may be one of the 'young old' in name but already feeling *way* older. She'll know these big family gatherings require intense negotiations and personalised efforts to ensure everyone has a good time. But beyond this, in our modern geriatric-friendly culture, she will be expected to oversee her festive program in a hospital-grade environment, with safe transport arrangements, individual diet-sensitive culinary offerings, ergonomic seating, easy bathroom access and sensitive temperature control to cater for the various frailties of the numerous elders. She will undoubtedly have a full medical kit on hand as a matter of course. Perhaps some medical training. After all, lives will be at stake. I know this: on two occasions Dad would have died at family lunches were it not for my brother Justin's proficiency in the Heimlich manoeuvre. Here's a tip: never serve prosciutto to anyone over eighty.

Sometimes I see myself becoming one of the ancient crones at my own family reunion—the one wearing the garish make-up and the outdated scarf—telling the same self-serving stories of her misspent youth that she has been telling everyone for *sixty* years. Boring not one, not two, but three younger generations: a multi-generational bore.

But I need to be honest here and admit that this scenario is still rather too optimistic, because I am probably imagining myself as a crone who can still get around, put on lipstick and talk too much. The fact is people can be kept alive for many years in a state of severe infirmity. I'd rather that wasn't me.

For those in or near retirement right now, advances in medical science and public health mean that we are better educated about the health risks we face and certainly better equipped to protect ourselves from those risks. But whether or not we protect our good health, there will still be all those medical interventions to keep us alive in poor health when the time comes. It's bad enough for those enduring it themselves, but it's even harder for others. We can see this unfolding in domestic tragedies right now. Lives and dreams are curtailed as the children of long-lived elders shoulder the emotional and physical burden of their seemingly time-unlimited duty to their parents, even as they juggle various other duties, including jobs, spouses and children. And, in the process, they now accrue the scars of sad, stressful and sometimes horrific experiences.

Annie, for example, works full-time and lives next door to her 90-year-old mother and father. They are both frail, and her mother has dementia. A government-funded carer turns up a couple of times a week to help out, but Annie cooks all their meals, and her mother won't let anyone else shower her. Recently her mother fell over and pulled her father down with her. Annie found them both on the floor. Yet another day spent in emergency; mercifully they suffered no serious injuries, although Annie would still have panic flashbacks and adrenaline surges for days. Now they await the next crisis. It will follow much the same pattern; there seems to be no end to it. Annie loves her parents. At the same time, she earnestly wishes them gone.

Sophia's Italian parents are living apart in two different aged care facilities. That's because her violently demented mother was so abusive to the Italian-speaking staff that she had to be moved to an environment where her carers couldn't understand her when she taunted them for being ugly and fat. Sophia works full-time but she devotes each full weekend plus many mid-week evenings to shuttling between her increasingly disoriented, incoherent father and her out-of-control mother. Her life has always been shaped by the needs of her migrant parents: as a girl, Sophia was taken out of school to look after her sick younger brother. She was long sustained by the prospect that one day, after her parents died, she would be free to live and work and find love in the Europe they had left. Today her hair is thin and silvering and her dream of a different life seems to have dissolved. She says with a sad laugh that she will be eligible to retire in a few years' time when she hasn't even had her chance to live.

Mary is married to the only son of a brave single mother who brought him up in tough circumstances. Mary's mother-in-law lives around the corner and her loving son visits her every single day without fail. He wants to be there for his mother until the very end of her life, whenever that might be. Mary observes with increasing bitterness the seemingly limitless years of this obligation, with her marital life still revolving around her seemingly indestructible mother-in-law. She now goes defiantly, guiltily, on overseas holidays alone.

Bettina finally visited a therapist in despair as she agonised over how completely untenable her life had become. She was not only trying to fulfil all the usual obligations to her work, children and marriage but also providing on-call support for her father, who was intent on living out his years 'in dignity' in his home. Hours were spent feeding him, cleaning him and cleaning up after him, trying to protect him from harm. No one cared about Bettina's 'dignity', of course. Or her sanity. Luckily her therapist was blunt. She told Bettina that her depression and anxiety were so extreme that it was clearly now a choice between her life or her father's. She told Bettina to 'withdraw support' from her father because only then would he accept the need to go into aged care. Bettina is still trying to summon the courage to do this.

John is the third son of a large family. A single man, he lives in the family home in regional South Australia and takes care of his parents, now both in their nineties. His smart, once active mother was recently advised by her doctor that she needed to have a heart operation. She didn't want to; she said she was at peace and ready to die. A family conference was held and the assembled children explained to their mother that if she didn't have the operation, she would very soon lose her basic mobility (to move from bed to bathroom and back again) and John would no longer be able to care for her; she would have to leave her home and husband and go into aged care. So their mother reluctantly agreed to the operation. Now she's back home after the operation—deemed successful despite various post-operative infections and associated cures that ricocheted into further ghastly side effects—and her children are surprised and worried by her long silences and lack of interest in life. She is at the mercy of the medical system and of her own devotion to family. Meanwhile John soldiers on.

It is mostly women who shoulder the caring burden. As Atul Gawande writes in *Being Mortal*, having 'at least one daughter seems to be crucial to the amount of help you will receive' in old age. Haider Warraich backs this up in *Modern Death*, noting 'the overwhelming majority of caregivers are female and 85% of them are related to the patient'.

I see so many of them: mature women who feel they can't travel, can't move cities or countries, can't even slow down and grow old themselves, because of their prolonged duties to their parents. More than a few of them don't know that they are subconsciously waiting until their mother or father dies before they can finally come out or quit their job or get divorced or even just dye their hair pink. Their parents will need to die before they can fully live.

What I want to say to women feeling guiltily resentful about their onerous daughterly duties is that this is a *new* phenomenon. People wrongly imagine (or are encouraged to believe) that their own mothers and grandmothers provided the same level of care for their parents as they declined, living on for many years in increasing frailty before they died. But that's not quite true. In the past, older people tended to be quite well until they fell ill, in which case they either recovered or died: quickly. They endured a sad but relatively brief decline, not the twelve long years of end-of-life debility confronted by the elderly and their carers today.

My mum and dad did not have their parents live with them, nor were they by their parents' side at their deathbeds. Nanna was still running her farm near Coonabarabran in Central New South Wales when she took ill, I think in her early seventies. She came down to Prince Alfred Hospital in Sydney for an operation and died there three weeks later, possibly of a heart attack brought on by complications after a surgery. The hospital rang Clare at 3 am to tell her. A few years later my two rural aunts put Nanna's husband, my maternal grandfather, into a nursing home (against his wishes) when he became too frail to stay alone at the farm; they were worried he'd stumble while using the big fireplace in the kitchen and set the house and himself alight. They had no intention of looking after him themselves and it was in the nursing home that he soon died. My paternal English grandfather, a pipe smoker and survivor of two world wars, 'dropped dead'—as they once used to—of a heart attack. I recall no evidence of guilt or self-torture about these events; just pragmatic acceptance that this was how life and death unfolded.

My dad, Michael, worked as a butcher until he was 70 years old. He was always kindly, vague, modest and lovable. When he turned 85, his personality started to change. By then he'd been treated for, and survived, several bouts of cancer, a stroke, a heart attack, water on the brain, a broken pelvis with a bout of delirium caused by the morphine, a few more falls, life-threatening sepsis and encroaching peripheral neuropathy that turned his feet and hands into cold, clawed, semi-useless appendages.

On one of the numerous occasions that I took Dad, well into his eighties, to Mona Vale Hospital, he was suffering what was for him the comparatively minor issue of a groin hernia. By then he was so frail he had agreed to let me help him shower that morning, an experience that was almost unbearably lowering for him and caused me to cry with pity and grief in the kitchen afterwards. Still, his old bloke's bluster was impressive. When I wheeled that frail, blotchy, thin, aching old father of mine into the doctor's room, he sat up as straight as he could and confidently assured the young man that he had always been fit, was never ill and, despite this latest setback, had no major health problems. The doctor was not experienced enough in the ways of the medical poker face to hide his plain astonishment at this ludicrous proposition. Then he turned around to see the three enormous manila folders stacked with Dad's long and complicated medical history. When he lifted the folders up and turned back to face us, the pile was so high the doctor's face was half-obscured; he asked if we could give him a further fifteen minutes to review Dad's files. The poor guy faced the daunting task of coming up with a plan to treat Dad's current problem without particularly exacerbating any of the others. Part of me loved Dad for being such a madly optimistic old bugger, but more of me despaired of being able to help someone so determinedly blind to the reality of his own circumstances.

It was hard to see Dad decline into a kind of sub-King Lear: querulous, irresponsible, demanding, unreasonable. He hated being told to use his walking stick and wielded it as a tool of his resentment, one day poking his granddaughter in the back so hard that she cried. My brother yelled at Dad, and my mother followed her late-in-life coping strategy of not seeing what was happening.

Then there was the time I took Dad to the specialist eye doctor who asked him to look at the standard letters chart to test his eyesight. 'Why do *I* have to answer all the questions?' Dad complained, in the new whiny tone he'd acquired. The specialist looked at me. I shrugged and spread my hands in half-apology for my own father. If Dad was a poor man's King Lear, I was starting to feel like an unsaintly Cordelia.

As Dad's capacities declined, he developed the classic old man's passion: an attachment to the personal freedom represented by his car. Dad would disappear for hours, lose his way utterly, and be returned home by the police, an unrepentant old buffoon, his family exhaling with relief that he hadn't plunged the car through the glass shopfront at the chemist. When they finally took his licence off him, Dad accused my husband of conspiracy, muttering that his son-in-law was after his car. Er, no. But we did hear the story of one son who was so worried about his father's dangerous driving, and the prospect of manslaughter charges, that he called the cops and dobbed his father in anonymously. Admirable work.

I loved Dad and he loved me, so perhaps that is why I do not feel ashamed to say that I was relieved when he died. Is it wrong to say this? Dad's final years were difficult and traumatic for our family as well as genuinely awful for him. When Mum died a few years later, in 2022, it was far less difficult for all of us because she was calm and ready. At peace, as she told me. She gave me a smile of pure love as she lay dying.

What Mum had hated most was the feeling of being dependent, which she certainly was, even when living out her last three years in a perfectly good aged care facility. She needed me and Justin to act as her interpreters, advocates and companions, to take her and Dad to medical appointments, to help them get care for their teeth and ears and feet. Those in aged care without someone close by to champion their interests and love them as individuals are certainly more vulnerable and, inevitably, lonely.

It is a common human theme that good parents can never really rest for worrying about their children. But it seems to me that a reciprocal burden exists for good children. We are never entirely free from the psychic weight of our parents' needs, love and ambitions for us in our youth, and increasingly we now find ourselves taking on guardian-style responsibilities for them during their prolonged old age.

I finally understood the accumulated heaviness of the burden I had carried about a year after Clare died. At 59, I was at last an orphan, which meant I could turn off my phone each night. I woke up one day with the most complete feeling of creative liberty and personhood I'd ever experienced. That feeling has not left me since. I did my best to be a good child to my parents and fulfilled that role for, well, practically a lifetime. I was finally now free; free to write this. And I came to understand fully how hard it is for any child to realise the hopes and aspirations their parents have for them without, in some measure, knowingly or not, suppressing their own.

THE DARK SIDE OF THE MIRROR

What is completely ignored in the fanatical pro-longevity/anti-death doctrine is that we humans need death. It gives shape and form to our lives. It has a crystallising power. 'Death,' wrote Saul Bellow in his novel *Humboldt's Gift*, 'is the dark backing a mirror needs if we are to see anything.' But you wouldn't know it, with our doctors and legislators avoiding the tough discussions about dying and the tech bros and life hackers treating ageing as the enemy: a disease that must be fought at every turn. No wonder so many of us ordinary folk freak out at the very idea of human mortality.

In 2024, the internationally acclaimed writer Alice

Munro died aged 92. She'd had the luckiest and longest life any artist could have. Admired around the world, she had won pretty much every major literary award, including the Man Booker International Prize in 2009 and the Nobel Prize in Literature in 2013. It was around the time the Nobel was awarded that Munro developed dementia and stopped writing altogether. This was sad, of course, but by then she was in her eighties and, when she died, she would leave behind a legacy of cherished, award-winning work.

If you were judging by the distraught outpourings on social media following news of her death, however, you might have assumed Munro had been brutally murdered, cruelly cut down in her absolute artistic prime, with decades of unfulfilled writing potential still ahead of her. People were devastated; couldn't believe it. More than a few distraught fans addressed the dead author personally on social media: 'Thank you, Alice, we love you!' as if she were up there in heaven checking her socials with a mug of coffee. The tone was one of shock, as if someone should have alerted these people earlier to the fact that Alice Munro was a human and therefore bound, like all of us, to die sometime. And I repeat, she died peacefully aged *ninety-two*.

This reluctance to accept the reality of death can be seen in the now common and bemusing practice of speaking to the dead in public. At award ceremonies for athletes and actors, more than one prize winner will almost certainly be observed peering expectantly up into the rafters and personally thanking their dead mum, dad or grandpa, declaring with complete certainty that these dear departed are looking down on them fondly, presumably from some celestial seat in the upper tiers of the auditorium. *Thank you, Mum, I love you!* Apart from the sheer absurdity, it's the height of egoism, as if the dead have nothing better to do than hover about the living.

The faintly hysterical atmosphere around modern death and its rituals is so prevalent that I have reluctantly come to appreciate the rites of the dour traditional church funeral. With a predictable order of service, a Catholic funeral, to take one example, offers a framework and familiar rhythms within which deep private emotions can be protected. The congregation is passive and acquiescent amid the formal priestly dress and trappings, the candles and incense, the tuneless hymns, the blessedly time-limited eulogies from the podium. It sits and kneels and stands and sings. This is succeeded by an optional counter-event, 'the wake', which these days means a session in a nearby pub or club, where a few drinks pave the way for expressions of shared feelings and high emotions for those who want it.

Secular funerals, by contrast, have become 'life celebrations' that can take so long they require a full day off work. At one memorial I attended all those present were invited to take the microphone, if they wished, and spontaneously share a reminiscence about the deceased. Naturally those who were most sincerely mourning stayed silent, while a few showy blow-in types with only a limited connection to the dear departed grabbed the limelight.

Modern technology has also made it easy for family members to produce what feel like feature-length shows of the dear departed's life, complete with backing music. As you can imagine, when the deceased is old, as is now the norm, there is a long backstory to cover. Look, the first few minutes of the slide show (no film; this is older-generation record keeping) are very moving. The next little while is also fine; you sit and think lovingly about your friend. But after a while you find yourself passionately cursing Celine Dion as she warbles that her heart will go on. When that's followed by the wind beneath Barbra Streisand's wings you feel just about ready to top yourself.

But I get it. We humans have largely brought nature to its knees. We control and subjugate it to our human ends. Domination is so important to us that we are destroying our own earthly habitat. And yet, try as we might, we still haven't conquered human death. We are disarmed by it. In this secular age, we don't know what to do with it.

I was powerfully reminded of my own sheltered immunity from the material facts of modern death after my mother's funeral in 2022. As I wondered aloud at the delay between Mum's death in hospital and the time her body was released for her funeral, my friend, a hospital physiotherapist known for her frankness, said that it was probably because there were so many post-COVID deaths that there was a backlog. The morgues, she said, were full. Then she added casually that hundreds of bodies were now being stored around the city in freezer trucks. A sudden terrible image of Clare's body on a truck shelf in a car park came to my mind. I still have to force myself to dispel it. At the same time, I don't want to be shielded from reality; I want to deal with death. In this, at least, I take after Clare.

There are those for whom death is such a terrifying prospect they insist it's not going to happen to them at all. They rely on denial and delusion. These people are nearly always men. Or men of an older generation, at least. My dad, Michael, was one of those people. He would have scoffed at Saul Bellow's pretentious remarks about the value of death. They are the ones who don't want to fill out an Advance Care Directive because they cannot bear to acknowledge they may end up blind, deaf and bored in a nursing home. They say blithely that they'll probably 'just drop dead' or 'fall off the perch' when, as we all know, they won't, because the modern medical system won't let them. They might be perfectly sensible humans otherwise, but for some reason they turn into self-deluded fools when it comes to their own mortality. They are also more likely to refuse to make a will. And deny they need to use their walkers. And insist on driving.

Dementia complicates things still further. It's hard for people to recognise in its early stages in themselves or in others. One brilliant friend of my husband's used to say, only half-joking: 'If I ever get dementia, I will kill myself and I'll kill anyone who tries to stop me!' I realised he had dementia when he stayed at our place for a week's visit to Sydney from Perth. One morning I discovered him sitting packed and dressed on the couch in the dark at 2.30 am, waiting to be taken to the airport. Of course he didn't kill himself. He lived out his final five years in a nursing home, a heartbreaking simulacrum of his former self.

Our relationship to death should also have been transformed by our changing perceptions of what happens *after* death. Certainly, most of us no longer fear that we or our loved ones might confront cruel post-mortem punishments in some dreary purgatory or fiery hell, or reincarnation as a miserable cockroach. The worst that can happen in the afterlife these days is nothing. Anyone who has been sedated for an operation knows what it feels like to not-be for a while. It's really quite delightful. Personally, I have always enjoyed the temporary respite from myself. And the idea of a permanent vacation from my own restless consciousness is far from the worst fate

I can imagine.

But the larger point is that in culture and nature, we need death. The philosopher Martin Hägglund put death into an ethical context: 'The condition of our freedom . . . is that we understand ourselves as finite. Only in light of the apprehension that we will die, that our lifetime is indefinite but finite, can we ask ourselves what we ought to do with our lives and put ourselves at stake in our activities.'[7]

Perhaps their lack of respect for human mortality is why I find those boastful death-defying tech bros and self-absorbed 'life' hackers so paradoxically inhumane, so ultimately life-*denying*. In September 2025 the world saw and overheard two tyrants—Xi Jinping of China and Vladimir Putin of Russia—swapping advice on extracting healthy organs from others (by what ghoulish means they didn't specify) and implanting them inside their own selves to prolong their lives indefinitely, while Kim Jong Un of North Korea smirked alongside them. I saw men who had lost all contact with their own humanity, our shared animal frailty, the cycle of life on this blue planet. They were out to defeat their own mortality. Yet they smiled as they watched China's grand parade of weapons of mega-death.

In a 2023 podcast interview, British writer Zadie Smith was wise on this topic and more prophetic than even she could have imagined: 'Without death there are no ethics. It's an absolutely necessary thing . . . can you imagine Elon Musk eternally, for all time? It's a nightmare. So I know that death is a gift; without it this life would be a hell without end.'[8]

I also know that death can give rise to some extraordinary experiences, to moments of pure concentrated feeling. Grief. Relief. Love. Even hilarity.

When Dad, aged 90, lay dying after a fall in the back room of a Sydney hospital, with Mum, Justin and me by his bedside, we respected what we presumed would be his wish as a Catholic and asked the nurse if we could have a chaplain to give him the final sacrament.

Father Paul turned up 40 minutes later, somewhat breathless. A Polish priest in young middle age, he had large, surprised blue eyes, a skittish manner and a hospital form attached to a clipboard. When I thanked him for coming in to give Dad the last rites, he was quick to correct me. 'We don't call it the last rites anymore,' he said. 'It is now'—he paused for effect—'the Prayer of Healing.'

The surprised silence that followed this optimistic news was accentuated by another unnervingly long interval between Dad's poignant, death-approaching gasps.

My mother and brother and I clasped our hands together and bowed our heads as Father Paul draped the embroidered sash around his neck and opened his prayer book.

'Lord, we have gathered here in your name, and we ask you to be among us, to watch over our brother John . . .'

Hang on.

He continued, 'Lord Jesus Christ, you chose to share our human nature, to redeem all people, and to heal the sick. Look with compassion upon your servant John . . .'

I looked up. 'Um, it's Michael,' I said.

Father Paul was flustered. 'Pardon?'

'Michael—his name is Michael,' I said.

The priest looked at Mum and Justin. 'Are you sure?' He peered at his hospital paperwork. 'It says here his name is John.'

'We're quite sure,' said Clare calmly.

'Pretty sure,' said Jus.

My brother and I looked at each other and tightened our lips; this was no time for sibling mirth.

Father Paul pushed bravely onwards. 'Look with compassion upon your servant *Michael* . . . whom we have anointed in your name with this holy oil for the healing of his body and spirit.'

I was still with Dad at the end, an hour or two or five later. It was a privilege, just as they say. It was a privilege because, about five minutes before he died (or perhaps it was more than five minutes, or less, I couldn't tell), Dad's breathing changed noticeably. His face softened, and instead of trying to suck in the air with those little laboured gasps, he seemed to be tasting it, as if air were a flavour and his mouth was gently open to allow the sweetness of it to pass through him. And then, right at the last, Dad's lips worked very slightly as they always did when he was quietly pleased within himself; as if he were about to make a nutty joke or perhaps take that long-anticipated sip from a glass of cold white wine at the end of the day. And then his mouth stayed open and nothing happened and nothing happened and nothing happened. And I knew he was dead. I sat with him and rested the palm of my hand across his forehead and felt it cooling down.

Death plays its necessary part in a meaningful life. It gives us the capacity for ethics, and love, and sacrifice, and legacy. It gives us vulnerability and yes, dark comedy. And death is never completely final, is it? It just changes our relationships with the people who matter to us. We are intergenerational creatures, living and dying in waves, and carrying within us the voices of those who came before. The best we can do is leave the world with a peaceful heart and leave it in decent shape for those who come after us. So part of our duty, in this era, in our time, is to confront and manage the challenge of longevity itself.

SUCCESSION POSTPONED

There's a lot of talk about intergenerational matters these days, mostly in progressive political circles. Following the 2025 election victory, Australia's Labor government announced that it would be applying an 'intergenerational lens' to its policy considerations. Treasurer Jim Chalmers specifically talks about 'intergenerational equity'. And for good reason: because there isn't any. Instead, there is a major conflict of interest between the young and the old in Australian society right now that is exacerbated by our prolonged human longevity.

Well-off older Australians, living longer in their retirement, are motivated to protect, control and enjoy what they have accumulated. They rely on returns on their wealth, which means they like the high interest rates that negatively affect young borrowers and mortgage holders, and they hate the idea of taxes on capital gains even though the revenue might free up more money for child care or education. They have little stake in innovative stocks or daring ventures that might pay off in long-term jobs and opportunities for young people in our national economy. They prefer to invest directly, or indirectly via their super, in 'safe' dividend-paying stocks like the big four Australian banks and fossil fuel-dependent mining companies. Those who own rental properties oppose changes to negative gearing policies that would make housing less attractive to investors and therefore more available to home buyers. Public sector superannuation schemes vary, but public servants retiring on old-school schemes will have an impressive income for the rest of their life, making them largely immune to economic fluctuations.

In June 2025 on ABC News, economist Alan Kohler attacked the self-serving and 'ferocious' opposition to a sensible government proposal to make superannuation more equitable and sustainable by increasing the tax on superannuation earnings on balances above $3 million from 15 per cent to 30 per cent. As Kohler explained, it was John Howard's Liberal government that, in 2007, turned superannuation intended as security for workers into a tax haven for the rich, with more than two-thirds of super tax breaks flowing to the top 20 per cent of income earners. As a result, the cost of those tax breaks to the budget was now more than $50 billion and would soon *overtake* government expenditure on the age pension. The government did not cave in to multi-millionaire pressure entirely but conceded a modified version of its initial proposal.

Meanwhile, again in June 2025, economist Saul Eslake reported that home ownership for people aged between 25 and 34 had sunk from 61 per cent in the 1966 census to just 43 per cent in 2021: only one percentage point above home ownership levels in 1947, straight after the devastation of the Second World War. Think about that. Among 35- to 44-year-olds, home ownership had fallen from 75 per cent in 1981 to 61 per cent in 2021. And even among a relatively older generation of 45- to 54-year-olds, home ownership of 70 per cent in 2021 had dropped by 11 per cent from its peak of 81 per cent 30 years earlier.[9] This is a manifest failure of the Australian dream.

For more fortunate Australians, of course, the solution lies not in good social and economic policy, but the size of your family's wealth. As Kohler reminded his ABC viewers, while many countries tax inheritances to a lesser or greater extent (and from my reading that includes Germany, France, the US and the UK among many others), we in 'fair go' Australia actually *subsidise* inheritances. Australia has changed from a society in which every child had a fairly, if never totally, equal chance of achieving success in life to a fully-fledged 'inheritocracy' in which who you are and what you are capable of matters far less to your future than your family wealth.

Although I can report that even that seemingly fool-proof route to financial security can come up against longevity roadblocks. I heard third hand a bitter but enthralling story of one ancient Australian patriarch who is so rich he told his kids they will each inherit $30 million when he dies, and so controlling he won't trust any of them to have any of it in advance. One of his three sons, working in a government office, asked for some of that money to put his kids through the vastly expensive private school system. The old man refused, instead offering to lend him the money at 8 per cent interest, to be taken out of his share of the estate after his death. Telling himself, no doubt, that he was teaching the kid a thing or two about money and how the experts go about it. Also ensuring that he, the patriarch, retained his ongoing power over his children until the day he died. Some day.

In fact, of course, many older Australians do help out their kids while still enjoying the fruits of their comfortable retirement. The size of the anti-mass tourism demonstrations in the great cities and ports of Europe suggests that the good life for the middle class in their golden years consists of roaming the world for entertainment, or at least diversion. I sometimes wonder what these retirees are really looking for; perhaps they want to reward themselves for their years of work and sacrifice by saturating themselves in beautiful sights and experiences before they die. Certainly, no great work of art or world heritage site is safe from their inspection.

Their children, though grateful for the parental assistance, can't help but note their own dependent generational circumstances as their cost of living goes up, the environment deteriorates, house prices skyrocket and housing security declines. Meanwhile the older generation, lovingly or not, controls the purse strings and the power.

In February 2025, a third respected economist, Chris Richardson, plainly advocated bold new policy approaches on LinkedIn: 'We can and we should do all three: tax inheritances, reduce superannuation tax breaks and give incentives to get new housing supply. At the moment, we're failing on all three fronts. No wonder younger Australians are cheesed off . . .'

Young people have been pleading with us to do something about this situation for years. Written back in 2016, Jennifer Rayner's *Generation Less: How Australia is cheating the young* offered forensic proof that young people's suspicion that they were being thoroughly ripped off was well founded. Stable employment had been replaced by the gig economy, job insecurity and chronic underemployment.

Home ownership was increasingly unaffordable for younger Australians hoping to settle down and raise families. Career progress was much harder because anti-ageism legislation had meant the end of mandated retirements. Rayner piercingly described her own situation in academia, where 'the professors sat on in their named chairs; going nowhere and ensuring no one under them could either'.[10] She is describing an Australian culture that cannot honestly pride itself on a 'fair go' because it props up the rich and old and imposes hardship and lack of opportunity on the young and poor.

All these factors bring us to the strange generational state of affairs we see today: with young people 'apparently' unwilling to leave home, or floating between share houses, lacking focus and drive, frittering money away and letting Mum and Dad pay for too many things. In other words, failing to grow up. I suspect this extended juvenility is not about their personal deficiencies at all but about the society we have created—or failed to create—for them.

For the first time in our modern history, younger Australians quite reasonably assume they will not be better off than their parents. Most don't think they will even do *as well* as their parents. As Rayner says of their apparent fecklessness, 'It's not that young people spend because we don't know how to save. We spend because saving doesn't seem like it will get us anywhere.'

It is the very opposite of what should be happening,

and things need to change for the sake of the children and young people in your life and mine. I am confident that many will agree with me in principle about the need to find solutions to give young Australians more agency to shape for themselves a better future. But the fact of the matter is those who are old and rich and in charge don't want to let go. They like their power.

And this is visible across all spheres of national life.

Let's start at the very top. The Governance Institute of Australia's 2024 report on the composition of ASX 300 boards found there had been a significant *decline* in the percentage of board directors under the age of 50, while the number of board chairs of twenty years tenure and longer was actually *going up*.

These are the leaders tasked to guide our major national corporations successfully into the future, but they won't even promote healthy generational change in their own ranks. Our passionate anti-ageism culture has made this egregious position not only possible but socially acceptable. Of course, you could argue that the board-level age trend doesn't matter; the wise grey heads take care of governance, after all, and surely what really matters is getting the right dynamic, forward-looking CEO and management? In that case, perhaps it doesn't matter that the average age of an ASX 100 CEO has also *edged up* from 54 to 55 since 2014?

Some board directors do seek, accept and welcome generational handover, but they are genuine outliers. A businesswoman sitting on several major Australian boards told me that she had turned down more than a few invitations to consider new board positions that would require of her, for a responsible two-term contribution, an eight- or ten-year commitment. When she said she was not interested because she expected to retire before then, her peers were shocked. '*Retire?* Why on earth would you do that?'

We understand why they would rather not: corporate board life is very well compensated, especially at the largest and most prestigious companies. Who wouldn't be tempted by that ongoing money and status, not to mention all-expenses paid trips to the annual board meeting in London, so conveniently timed for Lord's or Wimbledon? Why wouldn't they hang on, assuring themselves that their wisdom and experience remain essential to good corporate governance? And let's conveniently ignore the evident failures in ethics by leading companies in Australia in recent years including: Optus (triple-zero failure leading to four deaths); Qantas (fined $90 million for illegally sacking more than 1800 ground staff during the COVID-19 pandemic); and supermarket chains Woolworths and Coles, against whom the Australian Competition and Consumer Commission took action for misleading consumers on prices of common products.

And it wasn't as if this realistic businesswoman was intent on disappearing into a retirement home to moulder. She wasn't planning to retire from life, just from corporate Australia. She will remain a valuable and valued citizen. She will still donate to cultural and other causes. She will continue to mentor young and rising women to take their place and shape Australia's future. But the default view at the aged summit of Australian life is that once you have a seat of power in this country, you are somehow entitled to hang on till grim death. Literally.

This failure of those in power to hand over to the next generation is a theme about as old as time, certainly as old as Hesiod's *Theogony* of around 700 BC, the tale of succession struggles among the gods.

Jesse Armstrong's TV series *Succession* is a modern take on the old problem: the younger generation's ambition to replace their elders and reshape the world and the older generation's stubborn refusal to give up its grip on power. *Succession* owes a considerable debt to Rupert Murdoch and his power games with and between three of his children—and an even bigger debt to Shakespeare, who was himself a fascinated student of succession, particularly of the royal kind. The old man in question in *Succession* is Logan Roy (Roy deriving, of course, from the French word for king), who has risen from poverty to build a vast global media empire, and the series portrays the gruesomely funny and wholly unedifying contest between three of Logan Roy's four children as they vie to succeed their father.

The third episode of the final season offers the bizarre spectacle of Logan Roy dying of natural causes on board his personal plane next to son-in-law Tom, husband of daughter Shiv. Tom provides live updates on Logan's death over the phone to Shiv and brothers Kendall and Roman as they attend their half-brother Connor's wedding. This paternal death is the long-anticipated event, the defining moment of transition to adulthood, in preparation for which the siblings have been scheming and plotting and dreaming for years. It's the dramatic climax the television audience has been waiting for. But when the life-changing moment finally arrives, the children are revealed once and for all as hopelessly unready and inadequate. The younger Roys dissolve into an incoherent muddle of stammering, babbling and indecision at the prospect of succeeding to adulthood at last. They are constrained by the memory of Logan Roy just as Hamlet was haunted by the ghost of his father, the king. Whatever clear and positive future Kendall, Shiv and Roman might once have envisaged for themselves, either within or outside Waystar Royco, it has already passed them by. Succession delayed too long has become succession denied altogether.

Some years back I worked on a speech for the head of the Small Business division of a major Australian bank and discovered that this scenario is not at all unrealistic: succession too long deferred really does pose problems, sometimes terminal ones, in this case for longstanding family businesses. The banker told me of his beloved clients, often post-Second World War migrants, who had heroically built successful small and medium-sized Australian businesses. He said these businesses were not adapting to the digital era because the ageing founders were unwilling to change a successful long-time business model based on bricks and mortar. They had been incredibly hard-working and successful over many years but now could not see or would not accept that trouble was looming. They needed to adapt their businesses for the future but could or would not.

Meanwhile, the sons and daughters of these founders, and eventually their grandchildren, had been brought up in the business and firmly told to prepare themselves to inherit and take charge. But these heirs were now getting older and older, waiting impotently for their opportunity to lead. Unless that younger generation was given its leadership opportunity soon, said the banker regretfully, technical disruption would surely defeat these ageing companies. The new generation would miss the opportunity to make the necessary innovations for the businesses to thrive. The inherent financial conservatism of the old founders, combined with their longevity, meant an existential risk to family businesses that had contributed so much to Australia.

The banker was depressed about the prospects for the individual businesses he had known and worked with and admired for years. But it was also clear to him that this particular cycle of decline had broader economic and social ramifications. Capital that could have been unlocked for investment and renewal, benefiting these families and the whole economy, was instead being wasted. And the next generation of talent was left waiting in vain for their opportunity to lead. There are plenty of Shivs, Kendalls and Romans in the real world too.

There's another part of our economy and society in which the old still hold an unusually high degree of power, and that is in what we might call the Land of Clubs. Not-for-profit clubs are an important and positive part of Australian life. There are a myriad of sporting clubs for interests like bowls, surf lifesaving and cricket. Workers clubs and ethnic community clubs are places of culture, community and enjoyment. There are clubs for special interests of just about any kind you can imagine, from automobiles to agriculture and wildlife, from books to astronomy.

Anyone who has ever been a member of a club, whether an informal book club or a club-of-necessity like the strata committee, knows the alarming degree of power that accrues to the volunteer who finds their life's meaning inside the club. That is the person who steps forward, looks around at a floundering, over-polite group of ditherers or a bunch of impossibly divided and semi-warring individuals, and comes up with a plan and a program that might not be to everyone's taste but is certainly to everyone's relief. Yes, they may be bossy, but at least there is order. Things are getting done. Lazy people like me are only too grateful for such driven people. And so they achieve prominence and secure their power.

But. Those who play leading roles in their clubs over a long period, even those who deserve to feel proud of their achievements, can also become attached to the prestige and power they have amassed. They like it, so they stick around. The risk with longevity, of course, is that clubs can get stuck in the time warp of the values, approaches and attitudes of the older membership that dominates the institution. And so those organisations invariably start to stultify.

Take Legacy and RSL clubs. These are important national institutions, created to serve the interests of veterans and their families. But for too many years, Vietnam War veterans were rejected and discriminated against by the RSL community because, in the eyes of the remaining First and Second World War veterans, those soldiers hadn't fought in a 'real' war, and the unpopularity of Australia's involvement in Vietnam risked casting a shadow over the reputation of the Australian armed forces more broadly.

The RSL finally woke up to its error, but only once many of those older veterans were dead. It wasn't until 2023, nearly 50 years after the end of the Vietnam War, that the president of the New South Wales branch, Ray James, made a public apology to those Vietnam veterans. People say our elders accrue wisdom. Perhaps so, but longevity also prolongs prejudice.

In a different vein, let's take a look at Australia's numerous agricultural societies, whose many activities include running annual agricultural shows. Here too, change is difficult to achieve. In one such club, senior qualified members—volunteers all—had the honour and responsibility of chairing the show committees: Dairy, Arts & Crafts, Domestic Animals, Cattle, Horticulture, Poultry and even Woodchopping. As you can imagine, these chairs had a long track record, built a strong powerbase and networks, and could see no good reason why they should not continue.

In this case, the generational challenge was for the society to engage younger farmers and graziers in the enterprise and ensure that agricultural shows stayed relevant to them and the modern Australian public. On that basis, it was decided that committee chairs would be required to resign their position once they reached 75 years of age—which, let's face it, is hardly a youthquake—when they would also lose their voting rights. (The administration was able to make this move because, as far as I am aware, volunteers are not covered by anti-discrimination legislation.) *Naturally* the organisation would always be grateful to these longstanding volunteers and respectful of their expertise. The outgoing chairs would *of course* be welcome to remain on their committee. And given their commitment to the ongoing vitality and relevance of their beloved institution, these members would *surely understand* how important it was to have generational change.

Reports so far suggest, however, that they do not, and this careful plan for intergenerational renewal is not going nearly as smoothly as hoped. Because—and by now you won't be surprised to hear it—the over-75s are not embracing their dethronement. There is dismay and dissent. And that is only making life harder for younger change-makers. Look, regret for lost prestige is understandable. These good people will have contributed freely and mightily to the success of their organisation over many years. But the organisational price that is paid lies in the alienation of a younger generation (those flighty 50-year olds, perhaps) who can bring much-needed renewal. Modernisation is hard at the best of times, but our new-found longevity makes this necessary process harder than ever.

Reading this, you might naively think none of this antiquated club culture has much to do with our daily lives. But conservatism and backward thinking, cloistered and nurtured in the bosoms of our clubs is not, alas, confined there. It leaks out. It spreads. It poisons.

Back in 2021, the all-male Australian Club in Sydney considered the proposition that women should be eligible to join their august institution. A radical idea, for them. I've actually been to the Australian Club several times, because women are tolerable as temporary guests, if they are signed in and accompanied at all times by a member, presumably so we don't lower the tone and start talking about our feelings. When you walk through the Australian Club's doors, you enter the comfortable world of old opinionated men, old (and very good) art and an atmosphere of a long-gone past, which is ironic give how many of its members, even in retirement, still insist on playing a highly influential role in modern Australian life. As for admitting women members, in a move that was worthy of Neanderthals, three-quarters of the 1500-odd Australian Club members voted no. And for good measure, the equally venerable all-male Melbourne Club went through the same process with the same outcome the following year.

Does this matter in the real world? It turns out it does. The members of those clubs are the same people who hold the big board directorates, who have a great deal of personal wealth, who wield influence across politics and private businesses. To have their attitudes visibly reinforced, even within the confines of their club, only confirms the validity of their prejudices and potentially has a spillover effect on broader society.

And in this case it did, further eroding the credibility of the fading Liberal Party of Australia. In a state of near terminal disarray in New South Wales, the Liberal Party under the then leadership of Peter Dutton, commissioned two old Liberal luminaries, Alan Stockdale and Richard Alston, as administrators to oversee the drawing up of new party rules. The aim was to give the apparently moribund Liberal Party the chance of a future. Instead, Alan Stockdale made the front pages in June 2025 having told a group of senior New South Wales Liberal women that they were now 'sufficiently assertive that we should be giving some thought to whether we need to protect men's involvement'.

In the ensuing uproar, Stockdale tried to pass this comment off as a joke. Of course no one believed that, especially when it was revealed that the individual Stockdale had appointed to rewrite the rules of the New South Wales party was none other than retired Federal Court judge Peter Graham KC, who had been a leading figure in the movement to prevent women from becoming members of the Australian Club. He had won that battle by reminding his fellow members in a ten-page letter that the club was 'a place where you could get away from bossy women'.

Think clubs don't matter? In the 2025 *Australian Financial Review* 'power list' there were no Liberal politicians in the top ten. None. We barely have a federal Opposition in this country, let alone a potential alternative government. A party of largely old men, they have completely lost touch with modernity.

The negative impact of generational power and prejudice on our whole society seems perfectly clear to me, but I admit I've been surprised by the number of friends and acquaintances of my age who are very far from corporate bigwigs or club dignitaries, but just as unwilling to entertain the idea of voluntary generational handover.

And when I say 'unwilling to entertain', what I really

mean is 'appalled by the prospect'. One friend exclaimed, 'Put those whining, self-obsessed Gen Z's in charge?' Another said, 'You're *not* becoming one of those boomer bashers!'

I'm not here to bash—but I am here to make succession fair and timely again.

A CONTRACT THROUGH TIME

So how can we think about intergenerational duty in a fair and clear-minded way? The most thoughtful commentator on this subject was the great eighteenth-century Anglo-Irish politician, Edmund Burke.

Burke believed every society or state reflected a contract through time; a contract that should be treated with 'reverence' precisely because it was not some transient phenomenon. Society, said Burke in his pamphlet *Reflections on the Revolution in France*, is 'a partnership in all science; a partnership in all art; a partnership in every virtue and in all perfection. As the ends of such a partnership cannot be obtained in many generations, it becomes a partnership not only between those who are living, but between those who are living, those who are dead, and those who are to be born.'

Given this 'intergenerational partnership', Burke thought no ruling generation should have unlimited authority. We ought instead to regard ourselves as stewards, as 'temporary possessors or life renters' of this world, taking our community into the future with caution and care. As life renters, we were honour-bound not to destroy the original fabric of our society or become too attracted to floating fashions, because then the whole chain and continuity of society risked being broken. And if that precious social and political chain through time was broken, Burke memorably warned, 'Men would become little better than the flies of a summer.'

It was this strong sense of intergenerational duty that led Burke, famously, to deplore the French Revolution. Handled well, it might have offered a sensible correction and modernisation of corrupt French social structures, practices and systems. Instead, it became a bloodbath with the wholesale abandonment of French culture, traditions and law. In that case, Burke thought, those life renters had failed to protect what he called the 'inheritance' the French people had received from their forebears. Upheaval of the scale enacted by those reckless revolutionaries meant those coming after them would receive 'a ruin instead of an habitation'.

Because of his outspoken opposition to the French Revolution, Burke is sometimes viewed as a conservative. He was far from it, although he was certainly anti-radical. Burke is better characterised as sensibly progressive. He believed in the right and duty of each generation to implement change. He also saw the value of critically examining the past, where 'a great volume is unrolled for our instruction, drawing the materials of future wisdom from the past errors and infirmities of mankind'. He thought each generation should take heed of those errors and infirmities to figure out what *not to do*, thus avoiding the continuation of failed policies and paving the way for new and better approaches.

That support for wise reform was why in 1776 Burke was a lonely progressive voice in the British Parliament backing the fledgling American republic. He viewed the American Revolution as a justified move against arbitrary power; a valid push for British-style liberty. Burke was on the right side of history there too.

A modern Edmund Burke would surely see our situation today as nothing less than an intergenerational crisis, with the unspoken contract of intergenerational fairness being radically undermined. The old are simply failing in their duty to the next generation. Importantly, Burke was also very clear that protecting the capacity for renewal was so important that it should not be left to chance. It was not enough to regard renewal in theory as a good thing or a good policy. He specifically reminded his readers: 'A state without the means of some change is without the means of its own conservation.' The capacity to change needs to be *built into* the system.

Democracy is that system, and for many years we have been able to take it for granted in countries like ours. Now authoritarianism is on the rise with the success of far-right parties in Europe and in Donald Trump's America. Dictatorships will always be inferior forms of government. They are shaped by the cult of one leading man backed by his cronies, and the longer the dictatorship lasts, the more damage is done. In the absence of regular free and fair elections, such states have no mechanism to effect orderly generational change, which is why disorderly change, sometimes revolutionary, becomes right and necessary.

Today longevity is cruelly prolonging the reign of too many modern dictators. Ayatollah Ali Khamenei, who is 86 years old, has ruled Iran since 1989. In that time, he has imposed a virulent theocracy, sponsored terrorism, and subjected the women of Iran to lives of exclusion and humiliation. I visited Tehran in the early 1990s and met a 24-year-old woman who was routinely harassed by the government's 'morality police' for her failure to adhere to the draconian dress code for women. She was jailed on one occasion for wearing a bikini at the beach. Today that vibrant young woman will be entering her sixties . . . and Khamenei is still in charge, ensuring the oppression of women in Iran is as unchanging, comprehensive and cruel as ever. China's Chairman Mao wrecked his country and its culture but died peacefully in his bed aged 82. Generals Stalin of Russia and Franco of Spain both died in office aged 73 and 74 respectively. One of the worst, Pol Pot in Cambodia, was finally removed from power aged 72, but only because by that time his health had declined to the point where he was mostly bedridden and lost effective control.

Now consider the extended life expectancy available to the modern dictator, who not only has access to modern surveillance and control regimes to suppress dissent but the latest health and medical resources to prolong their own lives. I have heard people speak with sadly deluded optimism about the approaching, even imminent demise of contemporary dictators like 72-year-old Vladimir Putin. *His face looks puffy: is that really him or just a stand-in? See that shaky left hand: he can't last all that much longer.* This is wishful thinking but also a lame excuse for passivity. In China, President Xi is just a year younger than Putin, and he could easily live another 30 years. As we saw in China's Victory Day Parade in December 2025, Putin and Xi are all too keen to take full advantage of the modern tools of longevity, including the implant of some quality human organs to refresh their decaying insides.

We can safely assume that many of today's most appalling regimes, run by the world's most awful villains, may well last even longer than might have once been expected and therefore inflict even more harm on their own and other populations.

A democratic system, by contrast, offers a peaceful mechanism to get rid of old ideas and install new ones, by the simple method of voting out ageing incumbents. Or so you might think. But longevity is also casting its long geriatric shadow over democratic politics—especially in the world's most powerful country, America, whose destiny matters very much to Australia.

When Donald Trump was voted out of office in 2020 most people thought he was finished. Done. He had been the oldest man ever elected to the office of president: 70 years of age at the time of his inauguration in 2017. But Joe Biden promptly broke that record—he was 78 years old when he was sworn in as president in 2021.

The 2024 presidential election could have been, and nearly was, another contest between these two now even-older men. Aged 82, Joe Biden was not prepared to admit he was too old to run, despite the manifest evidence of his physical and cognitive decline. The people around the president protected him and lied about his competency on the self-serving rationale that 'only Biden' could defeat

Trump. In their revelatory post-election book *Original Sin*, Jake Tapper and Alex Thompson laid out the cynical calculation made by Biden's aides: 'He just had to win and then he could disappear for four years—he'd only have to show proof of life every once in a while.'[11]

Finally, under pressure (having failed to recognise George Clooney, of all people, who was not only one of the world's most famous faces and a major Hollywood star but also a leading Democratic Party fundraiser), Joe Biden passed the candidate's baton to Kamala Harris. Too late. Donald Trump, again. Aged 79 at his presidential inauguration in 2025 and a menace not only to his own country but to the entire world. We are all living in the nightmare.

Here in Australia, we have a slightly different political issue. It's not that the age of our parliamentarians skews particularly old. In fact, the age profile of the federal Parliament is slowly trending downwards, with about 23 per cent of parliamentarians currently under 45 years of age. The problem lies in the numerical weight and political power of old people in our country.

Burke's ideal of society as a partnership between generations, where each new cohort is empowered to make responsible changes for a better present and future, depends for its efficacy on timely generational change. What happens if generational change is ever longer deferred? If deferred too long, progress is effectively frustrated, even denied altogether. This is why we need to be actively promoting generational change rather than waiting around for it to occur naturally. We need to get young people into decision-making roles in politics.

While it is good to see younger representatives in Parliament, we should also consider giving greater electoral power and proportional weight to those voters with the biggest stake in the future: young people. To do this, the voting age could be lowered from eighteen to sixteen. Young people in their final year of high school would see themselves as citizens with a role to play and encouraged to participate actively in our democracy, ideally allied to quality civics education in Australian schools. I would further suggest that voting be made optional for anyone over the age of 75 and in aged care homes. The aim is not to penalise or discount the value of the aged voters, but to give them the opportunity to pass the baton to a younger generation who will inherit the future and be responsible for shaping it.

Now, some may ask if generational handover as a concept is even relevant today. Surely it's unnecessary in this modern era, when teenagers are in many ways as worldly as 45-year-olds and seniors are out looking to get laid like teenagers?

If we look closer, however, we are reminded that we

humans are inevitably products of, and to some extent captives of, our times and the events we live through. The difference is dramatic when we compare the world views of those who grew up in times of war not peace, or times of plenty rather than poverty, or through an era of social progress rather than social failure. Inevitably, we are shaped by the values and prejudices created by our own experiences and shared with our peers. The longer we live, the longer we represent those experiences in the world, for better and worse. We may tell ourselves that we are more enlightened, that we can rise above our times and couldn't possibly be subject to ignorant outworn attitudes and prejudices, but I doubt it. And we express these unconscious attitudes and biases through family life, in business, in politics and right across our culture.

I saw something of this phenomenon in my own family. My mother Clare was a progressive thinker, a passionate supporter of Gough Whitlam and a genuine champion of multiculturalism. But she found herself strangely torn when Australia began revitalising its economic relations with a rising post-war Japan. Clare had been just nineteen years old when she married a serviceman who had been interned by the Japanese army in Papua New Guinea during the Second World War. As a result of his trauma, Jack was a deeply damaged individual and a violent alcoholic. Clare had no choice but to flee the marriage. Eventually she married

Michael, my father, but those old wounds inflicted on her were too deeply felt to be thrown over in a hurry. She didn't go so far as to raise her voice in support of the old RSL Club diggers, who were deeply opposed to engagement with Japan on the basis that this demeaned the trauma and sacrifice of so many Australians, but she personally resisted buying any of those new cheap and nifty Japanese products that were flooding into Australia.

Generational memory is a powerful thing. A shared traumatic event like war or even a natural disaster can hold people in its grasp long after the event has passed. This is why, even as a young child, I knew something important was happening that summer's day when a new Japanese transistor radio, with Norman May's familiar voice narrating the cricket, was placed on the front steps as Mum weeded the flower bed and Dad washed the car. When the Holdforths finally abandoned the old Australian Holden in the seventies and bought a snazzy silver-blue Japanese-made Datsun, it was clear that the war was finally over for Clare, as it was by then for most of Australia.

But still there were some who held out, nursing their anger until their death. And those feelings were and are entirely understandable. But what it offers to us is a lesson. Making the future always depends on coming to some accommodation with the past, and that's a lot easier when you are young and don't carry the baggage. The longer any particular cohort enjoys longevity, the higher the likelihood that their collective experiences and ingrained prejudices will influence their political choices and therefore electoral outcomes.

The Brexit vote of 2016 was a powerful recent demonstration of this phenomenon, revealing the enormous gap between the perspectives and perceived interests of the old versus those of the young in Britain. Older Britons viewed the world through the prism of their experiences of, and myth-making about, the Second World War. They were attached to memories not only of their stoic national fight for sovereignty and survival, but also of the utter failure of perfidious Europe to stand up for democracy and decency against Nazism and fascism. Young British people in 2016, on the other hand, quite reasonably thought the past was over and saw full membership of Europe as part of their own bright expansive future. After election day, polling carried out for Tory party donor Lord Ashcroft demonstrated the widely divergent political preferences determined by those differing generational attitudes: 73 per cent of voters under 25 wanted to stay in the EU, while 60 per cent of those aged over 65 wanted to leave. And as we know, with the weight of numbers and the weight of longevity, anti-Europe sentiments prevailed. Britain had voted for the past, not the future.

We see it here in Australia too. In 2023 a referendum

was held on a constitutional change to give Aboriginal and Torres Strait Islander Australians a Voice to Parliament. The results showed younger Australians were more likely to vote yes than older Australians, with those aged 18 to 24 years at the time of the referendum more than twice as likely to vote yes as those aged 75 years and over (58.6 per cent compared to 24.2 per cent). Again, old people, with the natural institutional conservatism of the aged, and no doubt in part shaped by the deeply racist attitudes of Australia's past, had prevailed.

We are seeing something of this process at work as we continue to fail to deal with climate change. The first big Conference of the Parties to the United Nations Framework Convention on Climate Change was held in Berlin way back in 1995. Greta Thunberg wasn't even born until eight years later.

It was in the summer of 2018, aged fifteen, that Thunberg held her first 'School Strike for Climate' outside the Swedish Parliament. She had seen the climate crisis with fresh eyes. Today Thunberg is 22 years old and, while efforts have been made to move the planet away from fossil fuels and towards renewable energy, the fact is that temperatures keep rising, extreme weather events have become more regular, species decline continues, and human survivability is ultimately reduced. Yet rather than fighting against it, we seem to be progressively 'acclimatising' ourselves to this new order.

Few things will irritate otherwise sensible older people more than a young middle-class poseur risking the integrity of a masterpiece by Van Gogh or Vermeer or Da Vinci by chucking paint or soup or sauce over its protective glass. It seems to me that the 'sensible' older people have got this wrong. The very point the activists are making is that you don't get to make art on a failed planet. These young people have refused to succumb to generational amnesia, and they aren't prepared to normalise climate change.

Our piecemeal approach to the climate change crisis is a consequence of Australia's democratic processes, the governments we select and the choices they make. We can give younger Australians a greater say in the making of our political choices, and we should. We older Australians should respect the wisdom of the Burkean view of intergenerational change and accept that we live in a partnership through time. We have a duty to younger generations, and our duty right now is to give younger Australians more power.

THE CASE FOR 'AGEISM'

Ageism today is classed as an attack on an individual's inalienable identity alongside discrimination on the basis of race or sex. The Commonwealth's Age Discrimination Act 2004, which backs up various state-based laws from the 1990s, explicitly protects individuals from discrimination on the basis of their age in employment, education, accommodation and the provision of goods and services. No one can be forced out of a job because of their age, except in very specific and defined circumstances. Permanent members of the Australian Defence Force, for example, must retire at the age of 60 and reservists at 65.

Anti-ageism legislation has, of course, been a godsend for ageing baby boomers. At the first sign of generational criticism, or even sensible policy suggestions in relation to generational handover, you will hear baby boomers hit back that this is nothing more than vile 'ageism', that egregious and unacceptable crime, a retrograde scourge in modern life.

But ageism is not strictly the same as other forms of discrimination. In the workplace, for example, sexism and racism are clearly wrong because they equate 'ability' with gender or racial characteristics that are immutable. Ageing, by contrast, is a process. Ageing means change, and ultimately it means a decline in capability. That's just a fact, especially in this era of dementia. And what the baby boomers conveniently forget is that they themselves were once the most enthusiastic leaders in promoting ageism as a policy. In fact, it was only when baby boomers began to age, marvelling at their own ongoing fitness and vitality and relevance, that they had the profound revelation that ageism was a *really bad thing*.

These days we live with the consequences of our society's obsessive anti-ageism (by which I mean anti-*old*-ageism, because hardly anyone cares about ageism against the young) in some of our most consequential professions. Did you know that there is no statutory retirement age for airline pilots in Australia? I became alert to this when I found out that in the USA pilots are required to retire once they reach the age of 65. Hang on, what do they know that we don't? This American policy affects Australia's long-haul pilots; they are effectively out of a job once they hit 65, unless they transfer to domestic flying. But don't panic. The risks posed by older pilots flying in our anti-ageist Australia are mitigated because all Australian pilots over 60 are subject to six-monthly medical assessments conducted by specially trained independent doctors.

Now the move is on to raise the pilot flying age worldwide. Australia is listed as a co-sponsor of a 2024 International Civil Aviation Organization working paper, *Levering Technology and Oversight Activities to Assess Pilot Age Limit*, that questions the reliance on pilot age limits at all and calls for a 'more nuanced' understanding of pilot health and capabilities. The aim is not only to explore raising the age limit for pilots but to consider eradicating them altogether, 'emphasising standard performance assessment over age-based assumptions'. The reasons cited for this proposed new approach include advances in medical and aviation technologies, improvements in health outcomes and safety performance, and the shortage of pilots. (I guess investment in training a new generation of pilots has not occurred to them.) Naturally, 'discrimination and inclusion' considerations are also cited as drivers for this review. A representative of the Australian and International Pilots Association told me that there were many 'differing pilot opinions' on the topic of retirement age extension, often depending on which end of their career a pilot was placed. I can well imagine.

Now let us consider the case of our ageing health professionals. There is no mandatory retirement age for any of your medical practitioners, not your local GP, nor your specialist, anaesthetist, dentist or surgeon. In an ageing Australia, this matters. In 2012, an article in the *Medical Journal of Australia* observed that there were variations in individual ageing but warned that, overall, ageing practitioners were subject to age-related sensory and neurocognitive changes, including 'a decline in processing speed, reduced problem-solving ability and fluid intelligence, impaired hearing and sight and reduced manual dexterity'. As are we all.

The article went on: 'In terms of performance, older doctors are more likely to be investigated and disciplined by licensing bodies, more likely to be represented among those referred for competency assessments (specifically associated with cognitive impairment) and, according to most studies, perform worse than younger doctors in many areas. Years of clinical experience were negatively related to performance . . .'[12]

Today, continuing professional development programs for doctors are mandatory to support 'quality, lifelong learning for doctors that is relevant, effective and evidence-based'. Yet while doctors are expected to maintain good health and get a tick every now and then from their own friendly GP, there are no rigorous independent health checks like those routinely undertaken by Australian pilots over the age of 60. The only way an Australian health professional can be required to have their practice formally assessed by peers for conduct, health or performance is via an official complaints process, generally initiated by an unhappy patient or concerned colleague. In other words, once things are going wrong.

In August 2024, the Medical Board of Australia issued a call for submissions on a proposal to introduce mandatory health checks for late-career doctors, those aged 70 and over, so that they could make 'informed decisions about their health and practice' and 'manage the related risk to their patients'. The stimulus for this move was data showing that doctors aged 70 and over were *three times more likely* to be the subject of a complaint than those under 70. I gather this proposal has been met with vehement opposition from the Australian Medical Association and there's been no public news of it since.

Now you may be muttering that mine are the words of an outright ageist; one who fails to understand how our society is endlessly enriched by wisdom and experience. You would, of course, be wrong, but I don't need you to listen to me—because the baby boomers themselves, inventors of this modern employment system that vigorously protects the old guard against the advance of the new, were once in full agreement. Baby boomers were not always so humbly grateful for the wisdom and experience of their elders, begging them to stay in charge and retire only at their leisure, if at all. Quite the opposite. They wanted to turf all the silly old buggers off the bench. Which, in fact, they did.

In 1976, when the first cohort of baby boomers was in their early thirties, a federal parliamentary committee recommended *an end to the life tenure* of High Court and all federal judges. This was a dramatic moment. A youthquake. A takedown of the great and the good.

And where would they find those new judges with fresh social attitudes? Among the baby boomers, of course, although in the short term the immediate beneficiaries would have been the younger members of the Silent Generation. But the baby boomers had a long-term plan. They were intent on reshaping Australia, and to do so they needed control over the highest court in the land. They aimed to wrest the major decisions out of the hands of those old men (I say 'men' here advisedly) who represented the values of the past, not the future.

To understand the strength of baby boomers' feelings about the extreme redundancy of their elders, it's worth setting out in detail the invigoratingly *ageist* basis of their reasoning. Here is the full case for generational change in the exact words of the Senate committee, starting with that dramatic opening salvo: 'It is necessary to maintain *vigorous and dynamic* courts, which require the input of *new and younger* judges who will bring to the bench *new ideas* and *fresh social attitudes*.' (The italics are mine.)

Strong words already. And here is my translation of that official language: 'We need to throw out these conservative old bastards and replace them with young, vital, energised judges like us who will reflect our dynamic society with its evolving standards.'

Their words: 'The relatively high average age of federal judges does . . . limit the opportunity for *able legal practitioners* to serve . . . while at the *peak of their professional abilities . . .*' My translation: 'We currently have too many old duffers with fading brainpower doing an inferior job when we should have smart vital young people like us running the show.'

Their words: 'The introduction of a compulsory retiring age may result in the automatic removal of judges still capable of some years of service . . .' My translation: 'Yes, we acknowledge there *may* be some competent judges who are forced to retire before their time is up. We doubt it. But if so, too bad.'

And finally, the outright threat: '. . . but it will avoid *the unfortunate necessity* of removing a judge who, by reasons of *declining health*, ought not to continue in office, but who is *unwilling to resign*.' My translation: 'If you don't back these laws, we will publicly humiliate individual judges. We will force them to retire and make it clear that we are doing so because they are demented, dangerous old fools who reduce community confidence in our entire legal system and thus degrade our democracy.'

Personally, I have a lot of sympathy with the thinking of those once forward-looking Australian baby boomers of the 1970s. Did it not make sense to have rational methods for the handover of power from one generation to the next, especially where this involved the decisions being made by Australia's highest court?

Australia at the time agreed with them too. In fact, the impeccable logic of this argument led to the 1977 referendum proposing a compulsory retirement age of 70 years for all Justices of the High Court and indeed for all federal courts. A massive 80 per cent of Australian voters supported that change and enshrined it in section 72 of our Constitution: the biggest YES in our history. This was a radical takedown of the old hierarchy, a complete repudiation of the idea that older people should automatically be respected, consulted and revered. It was a huge vote *in favour of* ageism.

If it made sense then, why does it not make sense now?

The only reason to claim it doesn't make sense now

is because it is the baby boomers themselves who are in charge, and God knows *they* don't want to hand over power.

This is why, for some years now, the finest legal minds of their generation have been trying to figure how to get around section 72 to enable federal judges to stay on their high benches for as long they are physically and mentally capable, or at least as long as they are deemed so, or perhaps still more accurately, as long as they are not explicitly deemed 'unable' to discharge their duties. Ironic, isn't it, that the baby boomers in this instance were undone by their own effectiveness? They baked their ageism into our Constitutional pie and it's no easy matter to deconstruct it.

Meanwhile, the state legislatures, with more freedom to regain their privileges, have been busy in the same cause. In New South Wales, for example, the retirement age for judges and magistrates was raised from 72 to 75 in 2018—in order, it was claimed, to keep 'judicial talent' on the bench. Attorney-General Mark Speakman said at the time that this would allow the justice system to 'harness the judicial expertise of our finest legal minds for longer'. A few brave souls queried this move and argued against making the legislation retrospective, saying it would now take even longer to make inroads into the overwhelmingly white and male composition of the state judiciary, replacing it with a truly inclusive and diverse judiciary, more fully reflective of the society over which they had jurisdiction. Naturally this argument was not accepted.

I would argue that our state judiciaries should instead be following the excellent example of the High Court and institute a mandatory retirement age for judges which can only be overridden through short-term contracts for individuals of exceptional merit.

What we know is this: if we leave it up to personal self-assessment, almost no one recognises when it's their own time to quit. Even the wisest humans have succumbed to the myth of their own necessity, long after their use-by date. 'Those who have been once intoxicated with power, and have derived any kind of emolument from it, even though for but one year, can never willingly abandon it,' observed wise Edmund Burke in 1791.

And the consequences of this self-centredness can be devastating. Let's remind ourselves of the notorious case of the eminent American jurist Ruth Bader Ginsburg. In 1993, aged 60, Ginsburg was appointed to the seven-member United States Supreme Court. She was nominated by President Bill Clinton with her appointment heartily approved, as required, by the Senate, which was then held by the Democrats. According to Section 1, Article 3 of the United States Constitution, dating back to 1789, there are no term limits: 'The Judges, both of the supreme and inferior Courts, shall hold their Offices during good Behaviour . . .' That provision has never been changed. It's a job for life, if you want it.

By 2014, Ruth Bader Ginsburg had been on the bench for 21 years. She was now 81 years old and had recovered after treatment from several bouts of cancer and associated side effects. At that time, President Obama was completing his second and final term as president and the Democrats still held that precious majority in the Senate. If Ginsburg stepped down at that moment, the president would have the opportunity to appoint her replacement and thereby secure a progressive majority on the Supreme Court for a long, long time to come: a political prize beyond rubies in the US system. But Ginsburg ignored the public pleas and the private hints, including from President Obama himself, to step down while the going was good. She was a woman hitherto renowned for being sensible and unsentimental, but she had succumbed like so many others to the self-delusion peculiar to old age. She was essential. Also, she liked the job. She refused to quit.

Her reasoning was never made public, but the kindest explanation is that Ginsburg believed Hillary Clinton would win the 2016 election and Ginsburg could then retire at some point during the Clinton presidency. Well, she was wrong about that. To be even kinder to Ginsburg, we could presume that she calculated that if worse came to worst and the ageing Donald Trump was elected president, she would stay alive long enough to outlast him. She was wrong there too.

Donald Trump won that election in 2016, and in 2018 the Senate turned conservative. Ruth Bader Ginsburg died aged 87 in late 2020, right at the very end of Trump's presidency. This gave the outgoing President Trump just enough time to move forward with his own pick for replacement, the conservative Justice Amy Coney Barrett, who was waved through by the conservative majority Senate, thus assuring a job-for-life conservative majority on the Supreme Court.

Did Ginsburg's attachment to her own status, ego and pride in her personal judgement matter? Yes. In that conservative-stacked Supreme Court, Justice Amy Coney Barrett went on to cast the deciding vote that overturned the landmark Roe v. Wade abortion rights ruling less than two years later. Today, American women in conservative-run states all over the country are facing unbearable choices; they no longer retain rights over their own bodies, because Ginsburg made the wrong choice about her own.

The 2024 US election campaign was then won by Donald Trump. And we now know that Trump won, at least in part, because of 82-year-old President Biden's ego-driven failure to step aside in a timely manner. Joe Biden not only held on until the last minute but also took it upon himself to crown Kamala Harris as his heir apparent, without reference to any due internal Democratic Party process. It was an old man's last-ditch exercise of his political power. Meanwhile, long after the presidential election was lost, a wobbling and whispering Biden was still claiming he would have won if only those bastards hadn't forced him to stand down.

Which brings us back to the Australian baby boomers, an entire generation unwilling to cede their primary role in Australian life. Having once ousted the old guard based on their age, infirmity and decrepitude, the baby boomers took fright as soon as they spotted a few grey hairs of their own. They realised they were now at risk of being deposed in much the same ruthless way as they unseated their elders in 1977. Hence the Commonwealth's Age Discrimination Act 2004. Yes, where once the baby boomers were all in favour of youthful energy and progress, they had now, out of naked self-interest, discovered the benefits of experience and the wisdom of age. They have converted this into a full-blown moral crusade: how disgraceful, how wasteful, how downright wrong it would be to chuck our qualified seniors on the scrap heap! And their argument has worked. For a second time the baby boomers reshaped the entire system in their favour, this time by inventing the sin of ageism.

Our society has become so afraid of committing this sin that it is no longer taking commonsense precautions to protect the broader interests of all its citizens. I've mentioned examples like pilots, judges, surgeons and general practitioners. Now let me give you a more everyday example of the problems caused by our anti-ageism fetish. All over Australia right now, elderly people (mostly men) shamelessly insist on their right to drive, despite posing a danger to themselves and other road users, just as my late dad used to do. Every day there's another story of some old bloke veering off roads into bushes, fences, houses and shops. Once a month I see that a 'medical incident' is blamed for a serious or even fatal car accident, which is often code for some selfish old bugger deluding himself about his virile good health and therefore refusing to take his medication, before sitting behind the wheel of a lethal instrument, turning the engine on and pressing his foot on the accelerator.

Not long ago an 80-year-old driver rolled his car across three lanes of traffic in Sydney; almost inevitably his car was crashed into and he was killed. Yet again a 'medical incident' was blamed, as if this were some act of God rather than an entirely predictable product of age-related decline. My sympathies are with the driver of the other car, injured and no doubt traumatised by the experience.

Another recent and notable driving stuff-up, happily

less catastrophic, was precipitated because an old chap really did have a medical incident—a fall at home. On the day in question, he was supposed to be walking to his friend's house to be driven by his friend to a doctor who would check the state of his head. But this chap decided instead to *drive* to his friend's place. With his broken head. On the way there, he sped over a small urban cliff that no one had ever heard of, landed twelve metres below, and miraculously survived without badly injuring himself or anyone else. If he'd been a drunk teenager there would have been angst and outrage. As it was, in the story on the evening news, locals stood around admiring the wrecked car, thanking the rescuers and noting that 'it could have been worse' and 'these things happen'. I wonder what those tolerant neighbours will think once they realise what the behaviour of all these lovable old blokes is doing to their car insurance premiums.

Worst of all, a 60-something couple, walking their toddler grandson in Melbourne, were mown down on the footpath by a car driven by a 91-year-old woman.

These events should not be happening. There are, in theory, quite strict checks and balances in place regarding driving eligibility and these were updated and reinforced nationally in August 2025. But in today's fervid anti-ageism environment, in practice even authorised public servants like GPs and driving testers are understandably cautious about taking away an elderly driver's right to their licence. They hesitate before doing the necessary thing, which is to call out age-related infirmity and act on its implications to protect the public.

Certainly from age 80 to 88, Dad's driving became more of a danger to himself and others. Somehow, to our family's incredulity, he was allowed to keep his licence. Dad was so convinced of his genuine driving prowess that when he returned from what turned out to be his final test, he triumphantly threw the bit of paper on the table and boasted to Mum that he had been cleared to hit the road as usual. She couldn't believe it. She picked up the paper and read it. 'But Michael, this says you have failed.' Dad was at first disbelieving, because the examiner had obviously been too gutless to tell him the bad news in person, and ultimately devastated. We were sad for him but greatly relieved. Dad died a few months later and I have no doubt losing his licence hastened his final decline. But at least he didn't hurt himself or Mum or anyone else while he was still feeling good about himself on the road.

Meanwhile, we have now defined the crime of ageism so broadly that it has become almost impossible to use common sense and require older people to retire from any areas of modern life where continuing tenure is no longer appropriate, or where it would serve the broader society to give younger people the opportunity to contribute.

Even the most passionate defenders of anti-ageism can only make this argument on the debatable basis of the wisdom, caution and relevant experience of elders. But with longevity keeping old people in charge for longer and longer, our system is not fit for progress, innovation and communal safety.

We could consider removing all references to ageism in the various pieces of federal and state anti-discrimination legislation. In fact, this offence is rather hard to enforce because it's very difficult to prove, which is why online and in print you can find many anguished but impotent allegations that recruiters and employers are discriminating against older applicants. More importantly, this would reduce the modern bias *towards* the aged. It would promote open discussions between employers and older employees so that sensible planning for succession and workforce rejuvenation can be made.

We are conditioned by the anti-ageism lobby to think that our mental powers and reaction times don't decline with age, or if they do that the difference is miniscule. But that's not true. The Medical Board of Australia acknowledged, in its call for submissions on patient safety and late-career doctors in 2024, that 'there is an increased incidence of health impairment as individuals age'. Indeed.

This fact should be acknowledged without blame or shame but with a sense of realism. Increasingly, as we know, the risk is dementia, a disease which creeps up so invisibly and insidiously that the sufferer is often the last person to recognise they have it. So there is no excuse for professional organisations to permit professionals in their industry to control their own date of retirement. Not only does it block or hinder career opportunities for young and dynamic practitioners, it's improper, ineffective, it's unkind and it's probably dangerous. It's also unrealistic to expect colleagues to take on the responsibility of telling their peers they appear to be going dotty and it is time to retire.

The honest French essayist Michel de Montaigne, writing in his tower in sixteenth-century France, admitted to himself and to his readers that since he turned *thirty*, he felt his body and mind had decreased in power. Yes, he thought, ageing brought with it benefits such as experience and knowledge, but he felt the more important qualities of vitality, quickness and firmness had tended to droop and fade.

He wrote, 'Sometimes it is the body which is the first to surrender to old age, sometimes too the soul; and I have known plenty of men whose brains grew weak before their stomachs or their legs; and it is all the more dangerous an infirmity in that the sufferer is hardly aware of it and its symptoms are not clear ones.'[13] We should heed Montaigne and reinstitute ageism where it makes sense—for community safety—and for the sake of a well-functioning future.

THE HARD PRUNE

Generational change in any human society occurs when an older cohort retires, dies or is otherwise removed from power. You may say to me that you can have bad outcomes from generational change as well as good. Sure. You can get even worse outcomes when a corporate or political or familial regime hangs on for too long, resisting necessary change, ultimately guaranteeing upheaval or revolution. This last methodology is by no means ideal, of course. A revolutionary process can do more and faster, but the process is far less predictable and prone to missteps and shocks. Timely, steady generational turnover ensures the system can correct itself peaceably as it goes along.

Whatever the process, if you look at any period of history, across any field of human endeavour, from science to politics, economics, the arts and culture, you will see that humanity's great turning points are only made possible when new leaders with new ideas arise from a younger generation. Gardeners call this a *hard prune*, getting rid of the old growth to nurture the young sprigs. Just as the phoenix is reborn from its own ashes, so the advance of human civilisation and progress is facilitated, even accelerated, when one generation gives way to the next.

It is young people, with no sentimental or vested interest in the past, who will most readily, even ruthlessly, overturn the old orthodoxies and create new realities. Take the American Revolution, when young America repudiated old Britain, that revolution whose aims Edmund Burke endorsed. We think of the founding fathers as venerable old men but in fact it was a young man's game. Thomas Jefferson was 33 years old when he wrote the Declaration of Independence. The average age of the signers of the Declaration was 44, and more than a dozen of them were 35 or younger: Alexander Hamilton was 21 and James Monroe was just 18. Contrast that with today's Washington: one decrepit old American president after another, and the US Senate described by former presidential candidate Nikki Haley as 'the most privileged nursing home in the country'.

Then there's the French Revolution, a classic case of upheaval driven by youth, made inevitable by the old regime's stubborn resistance to change. By the time the key French radical leader Maximilien Robespierre reached the age of 36, he had been a leading extremist figure in the French Revolution, deposed the Crown, executed the King and Queen, and had his own head cut off by a new generation of counter-revolutionary forces (because counter-revolutions are also the preserve of the young).

When Napoleon Bonaparte stepped in to restore order to a chaotic post-Revolutionary France, he implemented vital civil reforms, shaped the legal system that is still the basis of French society today, and went on to conquer Europe before his downfall. He was a mere 30 years old when he became First Consul.

The most revolutionary conceptual leaps in business and science also belong to the young. Charles Darwin was 22 when he sailed on the famous *Beagle* to the Galápagos Islands and formulated new ideas about how species are formed. Steve Wozniak was 26 and Steve Jobs just 21 when they founded Apple. Einstein was 26 when he had his breakthrough year, known as the Miracle Year, with a series of insights into the nature of space and time that would change the world.

You will probably have heard the now-familiar phrase 'paradigm shift'. This elegant formula was coined in 1962 by a historian of science, Thomas Kuhn, in a book that itself constituted a paradigm shift. In *The Structure of Scientific Revolutions*, Kuhn unravelled the surprising process whereby a prevailing scientific framework or 'paradigm' is replaced by an entirely new framework of thinking.

Science normally proceeds inside the accepted intellectual paradigm of the day. Problems, findings and advances are all made within that well-established framework. From time to time, however, normal science hits some kind of obstacle: perhaps someone notices anomalies, or data that cannot be explained by prevailing assumptions, or a new and noteworthy puzzle emerges that is not susceptible to explanation via the current model. These glitches in the smooth working of the system demonstrate that the existing paradigm is no longer working effectively, and a new intellectual framework might be necessary. A period of instability may well ensue, and eventually there will be a crisis. That's because the old paradigm has broken down as a coherent explanation of reality, but no new paradigm has turned up to take its place.

Eventually, however, a new and better way is found to describe reality. Once the new paradigm is established, a new era of 'normal' science can flow. It is by this process that Isaac Newton's physics replaced Aristotle's classical paradigm, and quantum physics replaced Newtonian physics.

You might imagine that arriving at a 'paradigm shift' would involve the usual processes of scientific discovery. That scientists who observe anomalies or differences or puzzles would think carefully about them, come up with new ideas or theories, test those theories via experiments which would then be retested in the usual rigorous way by other scientists. If the results were consistent then they would be accepted, and a new intellectual and scientific order would be installed.

But Kuhn observed that this was *not* necessarily how major scientific advances occurred. In fact, he argued, a major breakthrough was more likely to occur when people new to the field brought their fresh eyes to the problem or, and even more importantly for this discussion, when the generation that had prospered (both intellectually and literally) under the old paradigm disappeared and was replaced by a younger generation less invested in the old, and more open to new ways of thinking.

Kuhn quoted German physicist Max Planck, who put it like this: 'A new scientific truth does not triumph by convincing its opponents and making them see the light, but rather because its opponents eventually die, and a new generation grows up that is familiar with it.' This insight was so powerful it was repeated and repackaged over time as Planck's law: 'Science only proceeds one funeral at a time.'[14] Kuhn said: 'Conversions will occur a few at a time until, after the last holdouts have died, the whole profession will again be practicing under a single, but now a different, paradigm.'

There we have it. The death of 'elders' is clearly identified as essential to advances in human knowledge. Planck and Kuhn are entirely unapologetic in their argument. Kuhn, in particular, reminds us that science is a human endeavour like any other, infused with all the hopes, dreams, prejudices and, of course, naked self-interest of any other field of human activity. The old guard settles in, they operate happily within a fixed world view, they enjoy their appointments and awards and sinecures, and they aren't keen on giving way to the new ideas owned, harnessed and exploited for honour or wealth by the next generation.

We also know from the long history of science that the big breakthroughs do not triumph purely via rational persuasion. In fact, rational persuasion is more often than not ignored, rejected or suppressed. Because of this, new science has sometimes been kept hidden from view altogether for fear of reprisals.

I mentioned that Charles Darwin was aged 22 when he headed out as the resident naturalist on the round-the-world voyage of the HMS *Beagle* in December 1831. Having made the fateful visit to the Galápagos Islands (and pondered the curious case of the marsupials of Australia), Darwin returned to England in October 1836. There he immediately set about writing up his voyage and refining the groundbreaking theory that would be known as natural selection. You'd have thought Darwin would be confident to test his ideas in Britain in the 1830s and 40s, that globally dynamic and open intellectual marketplace in which technical and scientific innovation flourished. But Darwin hesitated, fearful in Christian Britain of a negative response from its scientific establishment.

Though Darwin kept working on his theories, he included nothing about them when he published his celebrated journal *The Voyage of the Beagle* in 1839. By 1842, Darwin had drafted a 35-page sketch of his theory of natural selection. He further expanded it in 1844, yet still he didn't publish it. In the 1845 reprint of his journal, he merely and coyly inserted this point, of the Galápagos Island finches: 'Seeing this gradation and diversity of structure in one small, intimately related group of birds, one might really fancy that from an original paucity of birds in this archipelago, one species had been taken and modified for different ends.' One might indeed. But he went no further than that.

It wasn't until 1859, when he heard another scientist was about to publish a similar argument, that Darwin finally found the belated courage to publish *On the Origin of Species*, the magisterial product of an idea he'd had more than 20 years earlier.

In concluding this paradigm-shifting masterwork, Darwin wrote:

> Although I am fully convinced of the truth of the views given in this volume . . . I by no means expect to convince experienced naturalists whose minds are stocked with a multitude of facts all viewed, during a long course of years, from a point of view directly opposite to mine . . . but I look with confidence to the future, to young and rising naturalists, who will be able to view both sides of the question with impartiality.

How about that swipe? The evolutionary scientist attributes the ultimate scientific virtues of impartiality and objectivity not to the stale old guard but to the clear-minded younger generation. It's a declaration of the value, of the necessity, of the *wisdom* of generational change.

You might expect that times have changed since Darwin feared to publish and particularly since Kuhn exposed the scale of paradigm resistance in his book, but the evidence is against you. A vivid Australian case study will suffice.

In 1981, a 30-year-old Kalgoorlie-born gastroenterologist named Dr Barry Marshall joined forces with his observant pathologist colleague, Dr Robin Warren, at Royal Perth Hospital. It was Robin Warren who, in 1979, had noticed something curious under his microscope: the presence of tiny bacteria in stomach sections along with the peptic ulcers that were being investigated. He wondered whether there was a degree of causation between these bacteria and the formation of these ulcers.

If this finding were proved to be true, it would be inconvenient for the medical establishment, to say the least. Gastric disorders like peptic ulcers were being treated then as products of poor lifestyle choices or temperamental conditions resulting from stress. Drug companies were making fortunes providing ulcer medications that alleviated a patient's symptoms for a time. When the painful symptoms renewed, as inevitably they did, the patient would be forced back to their specialist for yet another round of expenditure. What a pharmaceutical honey pot that was.

Gastroenterologists were also raking in the money doing repeat endoscopies on these same patients. Barry Marshall specifically noted numerous cases in which women returning to their doctors with a flare-up of symptoms were regarded as neurotic, told by their medical professionals that they didn't really have anything wrong with them, and offered antidepressants instead. The possibility of a bacterial cause for gastritis, and therefore a simple antibiotic cure, was never going to appeal for clear reasons of economic self-interest if nothing else.

Still, Barry Marshall and Robin Warren persisted. Marshall reviewed the medical literature, and he and Robin Warren conducted the experiments. By 1982, Warren and Marshall had discovered that certain bacteria were causing a proportion of gastritis or peptic ulcers. The elimination of these bacteria, therefore, would provide a cure, which is where the use of antibiotics would come in. A great medical and scientific and therapeutic breakthrough was on the horizon.

When Marshall and Warren submitted their working paper laying out these findings for presentation at the Gastroenterology Society of Australia's annual meeting in 1983, their paper was rejected. When they asked why, they were told simply that there were many excellent applications and unfortunately their paper hadn't made the cut. When they then asked exactly how many applications had been submitted, they were told there had been 67 applications—for 64 places at the conference. Australia's medical science gatekeepers had, with all due objectivity, relegated the presentation of a future Nobel Prize-winning breakthrough to the bottom three out of 67 applications.

With the help of a few international colleagues,

however, the two scientists began sharing their ideas more widely with the international clinical community. In general, their findings were still met with scepticism and even criticism. Barry Marshall was called a 'brash young man' and 'a zealot'. He didn't disagree, by the way. Young revolutionaries can be irritatingly stubborn and self-possessed. But eventually the ideas were taken seriously enough that Marshall's fellow medical scientists sought to prove him wrong. In the process, some detractors came on board while other refutations fell by the wayside. Yet despite meeting the normal scientific standards, still the science was not accepted.

In 1985 the rash and impatient Australian proved one thing: he really was a zealot. Because Marshall then took the extreme measure of self-administering the bacterium. He became very ill indeed, and his wife was understandably furious when he finally admitted to her what he'd done. He then went ahead and cured himself with a regimen of antibiotics and bismuth salts. This wild experiment was highly criticised but undeniably fulfilled scientific requirements and was published in the *Medical Journal of Australia* in 1985.[15]

No doubt this showy piece of medical theatre irritated his colleagues, but as Marshall said of himself, 'I like to do things a little differently, buck the authority, try something out of the box.' And the revolutionary act worked. It was now impossible for the scientific establishment to ignore Warren and Marshall's discovery.

Today it is established science that certain gastric disorders are infectious diseases caused by the bacterium *Helicobacter pylori*. Scientists are now looking at increasing evidence for the role of this infection in gastric cancers. When the work of Warren and Marshal won the Nobel Prize in 2005, the citation explicitly described their work as a 'paradigm shift discovery' in a nod to the phenomenon described by Thomas Kuhn. My brother Justin would agree. When he went to his doctor with stomach troubles, he was sent for a quick and gentle 'puff' test that swiftly diagnosed the condition, and Justin was immediately put on medication that cured him, all thanks to that young ratbag Barry Marshall.

The 'scientific method' sounds like a terribly objective and foolproof process, doesn't it? But in reality it is not the coldly pure and rigorous methodology for testing ideas and making advances we believe it to be. It is ultimately a human endeavour like any other, relying on a system of gatekeepers whose job is to disprove the novel idea. These gatekeepers are inevitably the most senior practitioners and scientists. And the gatekeepers are inevitably elders in their profession who will be attached to the ideas and approaches they themselves have created. The older generation will resist and resist and resist because they are, consciously or unconsciously, aware that their own income, status and prestige depend on continuation of the old paradigm.

But if you still want further proof that new compelling information and evidence doesn't necessarily equate to action or change, in 2019 some economists decided to test Kuhn's theory, with illuminating results. Writing for the *American Economic Review* in 2019, Pierre Azoulay, Christian Fons-Rosen and Joshua S. Graff Zivin questioned Planck's thesis: was it true that science advances one funeral at a time?[16]

Their methodology was to examine whether the death of an eminent life scientist (whom they described variously as a luminary, star scientist or superstar in their field) led to the creation of new knowledge in that field of research. They conducted a survey using case studies from the 'premature' death of 452 eminent scientists—a premature death being defined as aged 61 or under. What they found was that the loss of a scientific superstar did indeed change the field and advance the cause of science. Interestingly, they said the blockage wasn't so much about the superstar scientist's attempts to 'bar' entry to the field while they were alive. The psychic weight imposed by eminent elders in the field meant this wasn't even necessary: the mere *prospect* of challenging a superstar served as a deterrent to nervous outsiders. In fact, the luminary's dominance was made more explicit and visible immediately after their death, because the cluster of collaborators and allies who had formed around the superstar in their defined field would use their privileged positions to 'limit access to funding or publication outlets to those outside the club' and 'stave off threats from intellectual outsiders'.

Because of this, the research found, after the superstar had died, the most important new ideas did not arise from the core field of research but rather from adjacent fields based on a different scientific body of work. Progress was ultimately restarted by this means, and the researchers concluded that, 'consistent with the contention by Planck, the loss of a luminary in the academic life sciences provides an opportunity for fields to evolve in novel directions that advance the scientific frontier'. In other words, *death advances progress.*

But the researchers added an important caveat to this finding. 'When frontier research requires access to expensive and highly-specialized capital equipment, as is sometimes the case in the physical sciences, the rules governing access to that capital are likely to favour succession by insiders.' This is significant because modern biotechnology has become highly capital-intensive, generally requiring access to high-performance computing, large-scale data-processing capabilities, artificial intelligence and 3D bioprinting. Access to this equipment—or barring access to it—will determine the extent to which young 21st-century scientists can make their breakthroughs.

The next wave of geniuses may find it even harder to rewrite the rules and change the world.

COMING TOGETHER

There are older Australians today who would be only too happy to hand over power to the next generation but do not feel financially secure enough to do so. For many younger baby boomers and Gen Xers and even millennials, 'retirement' is a prospect to be feared not anticipated, because a long retirement potentially means a long, long decline in their standard of living.

Through compulsory superannuation, successive governments have put economic responsibility for what is today an extended old age into the hands of many Australians who are not confidently equipped to manage it. I'm one of them.

Women have been and still are particularly vulnerable in this new environment. Like those who have taken a lot of time out of the workforce to have and care for their children. Or those who have worked all their lives in gig-economy jobs like the arts or hospitality. The many who served, and still serve, society in low-paid roles in aged care and child care.

A few years ago, a friend of mine was planning to retire from her moderately paid part-time university job in good health and with a modest pot of superannuation invested in Australian stocks. For the first time in her life, she started consciously monitoring her investments. She quickly realised that managing her super wisely was not a simple proposition. Was she investing in the right portfolio? What would happen if there were a major crash? She became so worried about the future she found she could not properly enjoy the present. If she went overseas to do some research, would that be a reckless waste of expenditure . . . or the proper way to conduct herself in a thriving retirement? Maybe she should she sell her house now while the market was strong? She began to fret about whether she could *afford* to live for another twenty or thirty years. She then looked around for work to add to her income but couldn't find any, and as her confidence and optimism declined, as the stress and fear weighed on her, she may in fact have become less employable. Or perhaps it was just that she, like so many, had been hit by the continuing contraction of university jobs. What could she do to ensure her money would last? And who would look after her if she made some poor financial decisions?

My friend, eminent, brilliant, prickly and beloved, killed herself one night. I don't know why. But I know that one factor weighing on her mind around that time was her gnawing, aching feeling of economic uncertainty about the future. It wasn't that she was living in a state of present-day Dickensian poverty. It was that panicky sense that she was all on her own as she aged, and that if she made just one wrong move she might slide into relative poverty and fall out of touch with her former life altogether.

A high degree of financial competence is now a precondition for the successful management of a long old age. No wonder we reportedly have this new phenomenon—this epidemic, in fact—of 'retirement anxiety', where retirees are so frightened they will run out of money that they don't heat their homes in winter and die with a tidy sum in the bank. This fear of 'running out' may be another factor leading people to stay on too long in the workforce, using anti-ageism legislation to their advantage and thereby keeping younger people locked out.

In response to this growing crisis of retiree confidence, in 2024 the Australian Parliament passed legislation requiring superannuation funds to offer affordable, tailored financial advice for people with 'less complex' needs. That sounds good, doesn't it? But when I went for an information session with my own super fund about my very simple circumstances and choices, I came away more confused than ever. The adviser told me with a patronising smile that retirement income planning was not that hard; it was just a matter of learning a new language. I felt like retorting that this was precisely the point: learning a new language to the point of fluency takes many years, especially for a woman who, heading into retirement, will almost certainly be heading into a life stage likely to include small or large cognitive and physical decline, just as she is burdened with more personal financial responsibility. It's 'all care and no responsibility' for the adviser but sheer worry and fright for the client.

Many of us, doomed to outlive our meagre superannuation, will be forced to rely in whole or part on the age pension. Retirement used to mean just that: citizens retired from public life to relative seclusion until their death soon after. When German chancellor Otto von Bismarck introduced the world's first age pension in Germany in the 1880s, it was only available to workers aged 70 and over, when most of those who qualified were conveniently dead. The pension wasn't so much a means of support for living a long life but a reward for the few who did.

The modern age pension model was also designed to sustain retirees over a comparatively short period. Today, however it is a mammoth 25- to 30-year business, potentially including that final twelve years lived in very poor health. People like to say you can't put a price on a life, but that's exactly what we are all required to do with our own.

The age pension for an Australian in September 2025 was a maximum of $1178 per fortnight for a single pensioner who owned no home or other major assets. This can be topped up with a rental allowance and potentially other supplements for those in need of them, but a base annual income of $30,646 is a recipe for hardship. And there's a good reason why.

Think about what is required for a decent retirement lasting 25 or more long years. Modern life is based on obsolescence and regular upgrades. Most retirees will easily outlive some or all of their fridges and washing machines, their coffee makers and vacuum cleaners. Computers and software and phones and printer will all need to be replaced or upgraded at some point, because being plugged in to the digital world is the price of entry to our cash-free economy, for online medical advice, banking, shopping and delivery, for useful information and government services. None of that is cheap.

Today a 65-year-old retiree will also need to budget for ongoing maintenance on deteriorating eyes, ears, feet and teeth, when many of these costs are not covered by Medicare. Homes may need to be modified for safe living, while provision will need to be made to pay for an increasing range of care needs and services as people age. Households with dementia sufferers will have a great many care needs. For those in reasonable health, ongoing subscriptions and streaming fees for news and entertainment will want to be kept up if retirees are to have any hope of sharing the same cultural landscape as their family and the rest of their community.

For the sake of equity, but also to reassure older Australians that their society cares about their ongoing welfare and social participation, we may need to rethink the age pension rate. With the rapid eradication of so many jobs, we may also need to reverse the trend and *lower* the age of access to the age pension to help those in their sixties or fifties who can no longer find work.

I know a separated 50-something mother who works in the arts: she's about to hunt yet again for rental accommodation in the expensive suburb in which she lives (for the sake of school continuity for her teenage child). She openly says she is barely clinging on in this changing Australian economy. I suspect many people like her won't warmly accept a political and social agenda focused on *giving a turn* to the 'next' generation until we have sorted out secure and safe retirements for them. It's entirely understandable.

The current federal government is taking some steps to correct this situation. As of July 2025, for example, the Commonwealth is paying superannuation on its Parental Leave Pay scheme: a change expected to benefit approximately 180,000 parents each year and increase the superannuation balances of women in retirement significantly over the long term.

There's also a larger societal matter to consider. Some people think it shouldn't matter if a small elite get richer in Australia while the rest merely struggle through. But rising economic inequality is a political problem. When a society bifurcates sharply along economic lines, as ours is increasingly doing, we end up with two very different realities in Australia, instead of one widely shared reality. Taken to extremes this makes a stable democracy difficult to sustain, as the United States is showing us today.

Which is why national moves to promote intergenerational fairness, that I strongly support, must be accompanied by measures that ensure less well-off, ageing Australians are not left behind.

A SANE AND BEAUTIFUL SOCIETY

Novelist Jeanette Winterson once wrote, 'I do not believe that art (all art) and beauty are separate, nor do I believe that either art or beauty are optional in a sane society.'[17]

Winterson was referring to literature and fine art, but her dictum applies to culture in the broadest sense, including music and languages, archaeology and history, politics and philosophy.

Like Winterson, I want to live in a sane society, one that is enlivened and refreshed and challenged by a flourishing artistic and intellectual culture. More than this, I'd like to be part of a generation that bequeaths that legacy to the next.

Art can happen almost anywhere, of course, but history tells us that certain conditions are particularly advantageous for creative work of all kinds: secure accommodation, private and shared spaces, sufficient funds to live and plenty of leisure time, and access to intellectual and cultural stimulation along with the discipline of good personal habits.

Writers crave solitude, but they also need like-minded companionship. Young artists like to live close to the competition and draw energy from each other. More than a few artists and creators in the nineteenth and twentieth centuries chose a semi-communal lifestyle in economical and congenial locations like Cornwall in England, the south of France and Hydra in Greece. In Australia, in the 1930s, the Heide circle of artists was shaped by and around wealthy couple John and Sunday Reed on their old dairy farm outside Melbourne.

There's no better example of how much a talented bunch of young people can achieve given the right circumstances, than the Bloomsbury Group who, by experimenting in life, art, politics, economics and ideas, ended up changing the world.

One of four siblings, Virginia Stephen was 22 years old when her father died in 1904; her mother had died years earlier. Her father Leslie had been an accomplished, needy, self-absorbed, late Victorian man of letters. His death at the age of 72 was essential to the birth of young Virginia's writing life. That's how she felt, anyway, writing in her diary in November 1928, a full 24 years after his death: 'Father's birthday. He would have been 96, yes, 96 today; & could have been 96, like other people one has known; but mercifully was not. His life would have entirely ended mine. What would have happened? No writing, no books; inconceivable.'[18]

She's talking here about the deadening weight of paternal judgement, I think, but let's not forget about the value of the monetary inheritance too. At a stretch, you could argue that the formation of the Bloomsbury Group depended on Leslie Stephen's death, because six months after he died in 1904, with cash in hand, 22-year-old Virginia Stephen and her three siblings, including 25-year-old visual artist Vanessa, gave up all pretence of mourning, abandoned their old life and started a new one in a five storey terrace at 46 Gordon Square in Bloomsbury. It was a share house on steroids.

'We were full of experiments and reforms,' Virginia wrote. 'We were going to do without table napkins . . . we were going to paint; to write; to have coffee after dinner instead of tea at nine o'clock. Everything was going to be new; everything was going to be different. Everything was on trial.' Big sister Vanessa remembered gleefully that in Bloomsbury they were 'young, all free, all beginning life in new surroundings, without elders to whom we had to account in any way . . .'

They abandoned all the conventional social duties of their age, like visiting the aged relatives and attending society functions. Young people: every social revolution's strike force. Given half a chance they are culture's hardest of hard pruners.

And so these young people were free to spend their days writing and painting, lunching out and loitering in bookshops. Virginia's older brother Thoby, who had recently been an undergraduate at Trinity College Cambridge, initiated regular 'Thursday evenings', inviting all his Cambridge friends around (male, of course, highly intelligent, although seriously lacking, Virginia noted, in 'physical splendour') for whisky, coffee, buns, cigarettes and philosophical conversation.

The visitors included publisher and Labour activist Leonard Woolf, who would marry Virginia; future art critic Clive Bell, who married Vanessa; the literary critic Desmond MacCarthy; mathematician Saxon Sydney-Turner; and writer and rebel historian Lytton Strachey. Deep associations and lifelong friendships were formed. Later Bloomsbury associates included artist Duncan Grant, economist Maynard Keynes, art rebel Roger Fry, the modernist poet T.S. Eliot, and novelist E.M. Forster.

These young people were engaged in a private revolution, an outright rejection of Victorian values: God and Church, the British Empire, the Victorian obsession with material things—the lot. And rejection of that entire system and the generation that embodied it meant they were able to open up, with absolute seriousness, to questions that still shape our lives today. In a world without God-given morals, what ethical rules should we live by? What does a 'good' life look like, anyway? How much are we shaped by gender or class, or even the 'spirit' of the historical moment into which we are born—and can we ever free ourselves from these constraints? To whom or what do we owe our final loyalty: to our friends, our parents, our ethics, or our country?

Think of Virginia Woolf's feminism (that ringing demand for 'a room of one's own'); Lytton Strachey's iconoclasm (his demolition of the faded old 'Eminent Victorians'); Roger Fry's introduction of artistic modernism to Britain; Maynard Keynes's invention of macroeconomics and an economic theory that promoted the welfare of the many, not just the few; and E.M. Forster's deep humanism ('only connect').

The Bloomsbury Group was a rare phenomenon. But we had our own more democratic version of the Bloomsbury lifestyle available to us here in Australia after the Second World War, when young people moved into group share houses in Australia's inner cities, even as the factories and their workers moved out to the suburbs. Once university became free, and when a part-time job was easy to find, a student could keep going quite easily month to month. There were places to congregate cheaply and regularly: at home with your four housemates, in pubs, in Italian cafes, at dance parties in cavernous warehouses, at art school shows and at university, where clubs were a vigorous part of campus life. An arts degree student had *a lot* of free time. Social routines were important too, like cheap B-grade movies on Tuesday nights and Sunday afternoons playing softball in the park.

In the early 1980s I lived in Sydney's Surry Hills during a great flowering of homegrown Australian music. Down the road was the Trade Union Club, where every touring band played, including a gothic Nick Cave with his Bad Seeds. The Triffids briefly lived nearby and Paul Kelly lived up the road, with a regular gig at the nearby Hopetoun Hotel. Australian books were being written, poems scribbled and film scripts were, at least reportedly, in progress. Some young artists from Melbourne's Roar group popped by early one morning; one of them climbed through my bedroom window. Today you can find their work in major galleries. Politics was happening, too, with anti-apartheid fundraisers, Women's Day marches and anti-nuclear protests.

The best bit was that we were out of the sightline of our parents and in the company of other young people. Well, that was also the worst bit: we were young, and therefore stupid. We annoyed each other. Our share houses were grotty. But that's why it was so powerfully formative for all of us. That world was by no means perfect, but it had a lot going for it. A great deal of Australian creativity was fostered there.

Today that rackety but expressive Australian lifestyle has been all but eradicated as a possibility for younger Australians. Education is no longer free. The cost of living is high. People live online now more than in person. Inner-city housing is prohibitively expensive and in short supply; there are no affordable five-bedroom rentals in Surry Hills these days. Our inner cities are so dead at night that (in Sydney, at least) there are programs underway to resuscitate them.

That's not to say art and books and music and films aren't being made; of course they are. And the plus side of our interconnected and online world is that talent can go global from anywhere, including here. But it's all a lot harder, and our culture loses out as a result.

This lack of a conducive environment is a clear barrier to contemporary Australian art-making and storytelling. Another barrier is the scourge of 'cancel culture', which is antithetical to art and free speech more broadly. In a high point of cancellation idiocy the Bendigo Writers Festival's attempt to impose a 'code of conduct' on participating writers in 2025 resulted in a mass withdrawal by the invited guests and a festival apparently so reduced, dismal and lacking in energy that the organisers called off the closing night party.

Meanwhile, we have no written constitutional right to freedom of speech in this country. Defamation law here has long erred in favour of the individual's right to their reputation over the public's right to know. Longevity defers free speech even longer because, as I may have pointed out, people don't die anymore. Especially not the rich and prominent people who live on for years in well-appointed retirement homes, like the legendary Lulworth House in Elizabeth Bay in Sydney (one-time abode, rumour has it, of at least one prime minister, New South Wales premier, university chancellor and Chief Justice of the state's Supreme Court, at least three of them simultaneously). Today, everywhere you look, there is someone important who isn't dead. So that only prolongs the silence and delays the writing of unvarnished history.

In 2021 public interest was ramped up as a defence to a defamation claim. But a recent test of that defence was not particularly promising for the future of free speech and expression in Australia. Can you think of a better example of public interest than the investigative journalism of Nick McKenzie and Chris Masters that uncovered the war crimes of Australian soldier Ben Roberts-Smith in Afghanistan? I thought not. But when Roberts-Smith sued for defamation in 2023 and lost, it was not because the defendants had proved their work was in the public interest, but rather that they had proved to the judge's satisfaction that the claims they made about Ben Roberts-Smith were true. The judge *could* have said the defendants had won the case on both grounds but did not.

Chris Masters and Nick McKenzie have spoken publicly about the personal toll and the 'chilling effect' of our arduous defamation regime on investigative journalism, which is such an important part of any sane society. It involves great cost and complexity, uncertainty and risk, even for the most scrupulous journalist. Millions of dollars are at stake these days, and any litigation process takes great journalists away from other investigative work. And all this matters to our culture because truth telling—timely truth telling—is what keeps us informed and spurs us to make the necessary changes for societal growth.

We can't know how many important political and business exposés have been put aside out of an abundance of caution until all the actors, major and minor, have finally done the decent thing and died. The truth *may* out, but that might be so long after the events concerned that it loses some of its vital cultural force. And so we all lose.

Finally, let us turn to the undeniable proof that some in Australia's elite institutions have completely lost sight of the value of the creative and intellectual life of this country. The Productivity Commission was set up in 1998 to advise the Australian government on economic issues and opportunities for reform. In August 2025, the Productivity Commission floated a proposal to amend the Copyright Act 1968 to include an 'exception for text and data mining'—an anodyne phrase. The rights of business owners in relation to their innovative technologies and trademarks would continue to be protected, but not the rights of writers to their intellectual property. This would allow big tech companies to train their artificial intelligence systems using Australian books without seeking permission from, or compensating, the copyright holder; that is, the writers. The report acknowledged without qualms that large AI models are already being trained on copyrighted materials without consent or compensation. Indeed. Two books of mine, along with thousands of books by other Australian writers, have been scooped up without permission or compensation to train Meta's artificial intelligence system. As a writer, all I have is my voice. My Australian voice.

I can't think of a bigger disincentive to any young Australian who wants to write books, who wants to lead a creative Australian life, than the knowledge that all your work, art, energy, idealism and insights could be just picked up and carried off without even a murmur. And I can't think of anything less 'productive' for Australia than diminishing the incentives for creativity in this country. The government, thankfully, did not accept that proposition, but it is an indictment on our country and culture that it was even floated by one of our most senior and influential government agencies.

The major impulse for me in writing this book is a concern about the contraction of opportunities for young Australians to grow, expand, prosper, create and contribute. To live the full Australian life with both security and opportunity—and for some, the chance to live a *creative* life that enriches us all and connects us to our history and stories and each other and, indeed, our future.

As Jeanette Winterson warned, 'If we do not encourage new work *now* [my italics] we will lose all touch with the work of the past we claim to love. If art is not living in a continuous present, it is living in a museum, only those working now complete the circuit between the past, present and future energies we call art.' We have an intergenerational duty, indeed a patriotic one, to ensure the next wave of thinkers and dreamers and creators get to contribute to our culture and inject something beautiful and new.

CONCLUSION: FULFILLING THE CONTRACT

What makes a good life? We will each have our own answer to that question. But surely it is not about scoring points in a longevity contest, going on and on no matter what.

For me a good life is one of personal fulfilment, which means having the opportunity to develop and use my talents, experience good and beautiful things, and give and receive love and friendship.

The writer and reader in me would also value a satisfying closure to my life story. Like Daniel Kahneman, I appreciate the psychological value of a good ending, not just for my own sake but for my loved ones who might otherwise have to deal with painful memories of my long decline or suffering. Which is why, if it feels right, I'd like the opportunity to end life on my own terms.

But a narrative of personal satisfaction and completion is still not enough for a worthy life story. That requires being a decent citizen and playing a constructive civic role—contributing to a society to be passed on in good shape to the next generation; ideally better than it was before; at the very least no worse. It is painful to contemplate that right now, in this regard, widespread failure seems likely.

Today many young people feel hopelessly locked out of home and job security; old people rule with an inevitable backward slant, our society is failing to grapple with economic and intergenerational inequality and climate change; and the very old aren't allowed to die with a feeling of autonomy and peace. It's not good enough for us merely to observe these phenomena when we could actively choose to manage them.

And though I am inclined to take a positive view of our chances of success at turning things around, I note that one speculative fiction writer is doing his best to remind us there might be big consequences for failure. In his eco-thriller *The Forcing*, published in 2023, Canadian-Australian Paul E. Hardisty imagines the North American future, maybe 30 or 40 years from now, or perhaps less, by which time the climate crisis has ravaged the planet.

Whole swathes of land have become uninhabitable due to rising sea levels, raging natural disasters and desertification. The air is poisoned. Ecological crisis has caused famine, and unliveable cities have been looted and abandoned. Mass migration to safer climes has led to wars for survival. The still relatively liveable Canada has become part of an expanded USA, and a revolutionary North American 'Government of Youth' has taken charge. This government is determined to make the old pay for their climate crimes and secure some kind of future for the young. The government has therefore declared that anyone born before 1989 is 'guilty' of climate change. When they turn 50 their property and assets are confiscated, and they are forcibly moved to labour camps in dusty Texas. And that's just the beginning . . .

Australia can and should be at the global forefront in facing up to this longevity phenomenon. We have been there before, with votes for women, compulsory voting, the secret ballot, shaping the United Nations and more. It's time to summon that positive energy again. We have a record as a people of seeing where the common good lies and advancing that good with energy and determination.

We now know that around 40 per cent of the projected increase in Australian government expenditure over the next 30-plus years will be due to demographic ageing. We know that one in twelve Australians over the age of 65 has dementia right now. And Australians are currently only rivalled by Americans for the duration of their end-of-life suffering, with an average of twelve long years of chronic ill health prior to death.

Modern death is no longer something metaphysical that happens to us by an act of God. It is a knowable process that we can and should manage. We can choose to move away from a focus on life at all costs towards a modern medical ethos of helping people to live well and die well too.

This means training GPs and specialists to talk to their patients honestly about their circumstances and eliminate costly, counterproductive and sometimes cruel overservicing. Governments must increase investment to promote good lifetime health, and to expand geriatric and palliative care services. It makes sense that we should have a right to die peacefully once we have completed our lives.

Our culture is set up today around anti-ageism policies that were designed to eliminate discrimination against all older people, but in fact discriminate *against* the young.

No doubt a factor in this is that our most powerful corporations are governed by boards that are getting older, not younger. Our business leaders, overly focused on their narrow, short-term interests, not the long-term national good, have failed to step forward in support of sensible options put forward by Australian economists (including a tax on inheritances and a reduction on tax concessions that benefit the elderly rich and their offspring) to stop the ongoing intergenerational theft that is underway. A fairer Australia won't impoverish anyone but will make our society and democracy stronger, and our economy too.

One concrete way to start moving to intergenerational fairness is to lower the voting age and bring young Australians into the decision-making framework of our democracy. They should have more power to shape the future they will inherit and the opportunity to play their own custodial role for the generations to come.

There is a responsible case for a reinstitution of qualified 'ageism', for safety reasons if nothing else. Professionals in key roles are permitted to age at work indefinitely without an orderly plan for retirement, or even thorough age-based scrutiny of their physical health and cognitive abilities. It is still seen as more important to maintain old people's 'right' to drive than to protect people from older drivers who should not be behind the wheel.

Meanwhile, ordinary working people are nervously looking to a vastly extended retirement with insufficient funds, having been handed the responsibility of managing their finances without adequate support. The age pension will need to be rethought in the context of ever longer retirements.

This is a new era, unlike any in human history, and

it's time to rethink the contours of a good life. Now is the moment to air our hopes and fears about this modern phenomenon of longevity, acknowledge the challenges, and speak honestly to each other about the hard and worthwhile matters of life, death and intergenerational duty. We can choose to let go of outdated thinking and wrong-headed taboos, and make the future happen, not let it happen to us.

When Edmund Burke wrote about an intergenerational 'contract through time' he was offering us all a form of immortality. What we do today will reverberate down through the generations. We can squander this time of ours. We can live with the careless, callous narcissism of the dictators and longevity tech bros. Or we can adopt the ideas and approaches that build a rational and fair society for ourselves and the next generation of Australians, and the one after that. And part of our own fulfilment in the closing phase of our individual lives will surely derive from our generosity to the Australians of the future, whom we will never know.

AUTHOR'S NOTE AND ACKNOWLEDGEMENTS

My love and thanks to Syd Hickman, Vicki Hastrich and Charlotte Wood; my agent Jane Novak, publisher Jane Palfreyman, editor Ali Lavau, and all the team at Simon & Schuster.

More information on the sources I have used is available at lucindaholdforth.com

ENDNOTES

1 These generational categories are only so useful, I know. But even if we discount them, I still wish to deny that I am a baby boomer. I was born in 1963 which makes me, I believe, part of a sub-boomer cohort known in America as Generation Jones. Those of us born between 1954 and 1965 have more in common with the ironic and depressed Gen X than the optimistic and rapacious baby boomers. They had the Vietnam War and Woodstock. We had high youth unemployment, HIV/AIDS and the Sex Pistols.

2 Dr Peter Attia, *Outlive: The science and art of longevity*, London: Penguin UK, 2023.

3 Caitlin Mahar, *The Good Death Through Time*, Melbourne: Melbourne University Press, 2023.

4 Haider Warraich, *Modern Death: How medicine changed the end of life*, New York: St Martin's Press, 2017.

5 Michael Cholbi, 'Freedom over death', *Aeon*, July 2025.

6 Dr Ranjana Srivastava, *A Better Death: Conversations about the art of living and dying well*, Sydney: Simon and Schuster Australia, 2019.

ENDNOTES

7 Martin Hägglund, *This Life: Secular faith and spiritual freedom*, London: Penguin Random House, 2019.

8 Talk Easy with Sam Fragos, 1 October 2023.

9 Saul Eslake, 'Australia's widening health gap and what to do about it', *Inside Story*, 3 June 2025.

10 Jennifer Rayner, *Generation Less: How Australia is cheating the young*, Melbourne: Redback, 2016.

11 Jake Tapper and Alex Thompson, *Original Sin: President Biden's decline, its cover-up, and his disastrous choice to run again*, New York: Penguin Random House, 2025.

12 George A Skowronski and Carmelle Peisah, 'The greying intensivist: ageing and medical practice—everyone's problem', *Medical Journal of Australia*, vol. 196, no. 8, 2012.

13 Michel de Montaigne, 'On the Length of Life', *The Essays: A Selection*, trans. MA Screech, London: Penguin, 2004.

14 Thomas S. Kuhn, *The Structure of Scientific Revolutions*, fourth edition, Chicago: University of Chicago Press, 2012.

15 B.J. Marshall, J.A. Armstrong, D.B. McGechie et al, 'Attempt to fulfill Koch's postulates for pyloric campylobacter', *Medical Journal of Australia*, vol. 142, no. 8, 1985.

16 P. Azoulay, C. Fons-Rosen, J.S.G. Zivin, 'Does science advance one funeral at a time?' *American Economic Review*, vol. 109, no. 8, 2019.

17 Jeanette Winterson, *Art Objects: Essays on Ecstasy and Effrontery*, London: Vintage, 1996.

18 Hermione Lee, *Virginia Woolf*, New York: Vintage, 1996.